A Compilation of the Work Sheets
of the Linguistic Atlas of
the United States and Canada
and Associated Projects

A Compilation of the Work Sheets of the Linguistic Atlas of the United States and Canada and Associated Projects

Second Edition

Edited by
Alva L. Davis
Raven I. McDavid, Jr.
Virginia G. McDavid

The University of Chicago Press   Chicago and London

Standard Book Number: 226-13806-2
Library of Congress Catalog Card Number: 78-100481

The University of Chicago Press, Chicago 60637
The University of Chicago Press, Ltd., London

Printed in the United States of America

Contents

Introduction vii
Preface to the Second Edition xi
Arrangement of Work Sheets xv
Work Sheets 1-1A through 105-106

Introduction

Since the Linguistic Atlas of the United States and Canada was inaugurated in 1930 under the sponsorship of the American Council of Learned Societies, the work sheets by which the field investigators have gathered their data have undergone various modifications. This compilation of the work sheets used by the Atlas and associated surveys illustrates the process by which the techniques of linguistic geography have been adapted to the complexities of terrain, climate, economic bases and social conditions in English-speaking North America.

The value of work sheets for gathering a body of comparable data was demonstrated by Gilliéron and Edmont in the Atlas Linguistique de France and by Jaberg and Jud in the Sprach - und Sachatlas des Italiens und Südschweiz. In preparing the work sheets for New England, Hans Kurath, Director of the Linguistic Atlas, utilized previous studies of selected groups of words, A. J. Ellis's 'Dialect Test' and 'Classified Word List,' and various articles in Dialect Notes and American Speech. After criticism by the A.C.L.S. Committee on the Linguistic Atlas--especially by C. H. Grandgent and J. S. Kenyon--and a preliminary field trial, the work sheets, arranged by topics, were mimeographed and put into the hands of the field workers; then, after six weeks' experience in the field, they were further revised. It is this revision by which the New England field work was done (1931-1933), and which was printed in the Handbook of the Linguistic Geography of New England (1939).

For the preliminary survey of the South Atlantic States (1933-34), Guy S. Lowman, Jr., the principal field investigator for the Atlas, used work sheets including most of the New England questions, to which were added many items reflecting economic, social and cultural conditions in the South. After the preliminary sampling, from Delmarva to Georgia, the Southern work sheets were cut down by eliminating less rewarding items, and used for the South Atlantic field work (1934-39, 1941-48). With slight modifications--restoring a few items from the New England work sheets and dropping some from the Southern set--these work sheets were also used for the field work in the Middle Atlantic States

(1938-41, 1948-49). The Southern work sheets, plus a few
of the items from the preliminary Southern survey, were
used by Dr. Hilda Jaffe in her study of the speech of
Carteret County, North Carolina (1965), and by Robert Van
Riper in his survey of Oklahoma (1960-   ).

Items of special importance had been identified for the
New England field work, so as to provide a set of short
work sheets for the situation where a field worker had to
take a selection of responses from a good informant who
could not spare the time for a full interview. Slightly
more than half the length of the long work sheets, they
could be covered in a long afternoon or evening by a skillful
field worker and an alert informant. Later a generalized
set of short work sheets, about 520 items, was compiled by
Kurath from the three longer versions used on the Atlantic
Seaboard. This set was used by Henry M. Alexander in the
Maritime Provinces (1939-41), by Mrs. Jane Daddow Hawkins
in the Hudson Valley (1938), and by Mrs. Madie Ward Barrett
in southeastern Alabama (1945-48). A further abridgment
of the short work sheets was used by Lowman for his survey
of Southern England (1937-38).

For preliminary work in the North-Central area (1938-40),
Albert H. Marckwardt, then of Michigan but now of Princeton,
added to the generalized short work sheets a few items
from the longer ones; A. L. Davis and R. I. McDavid, Jr.,
added others (1949), chiefly items which might help reveal
the boundary between North Midland and South Midland speech
in the states north of the Ohio River (With slight modifications this version was also used by Marvin Carmony in
his study of the speech of Terre Haute, Indiana, 1965). This
example was followed by those conducting surveys in other
regions: Harold B. Allen in the Upper Midwest, Marjorie
Kimmerle and her colleagues in the Rocky Mountain States,
H. R. Wilson for the new study of the Maritimes, E. B. Atwood
in Texas, David W. Reed on the Pacific Coast, E. R. Seary
and William Kirwin in Newfoundland, Lee Pederson in Chicago.
Some of these items represent the restoration of fruitful
items from the long work sheets; some are designed to explore
the characteristic terms for regional geographic, economic
and cultural features; a few represent fields which were
not investigated along the Atlantic Seaboard but which the
experience of field workers might have geographic or suggested
social variants. Each of the regional surveys has omitted
a few items from the generalized form of the short work
sheets which were found unrewarding in the physical or
cultural environment of a particular region.

The work sheets which C. M. Wise and his students used in Louisiana and Missouri (1936-61) are based on the enlarged form of the long work sheets which Lowman used for his preliminary investigation of the South, with the addition of numerous items significant for the Gulf States and Lower Mississippi Valley. A modification of these work sheets, with even greater attention to local culture and almost purely lexical in nature, was devised by John LeCompte for his study of the vocabulary of Lafourche Parish and Grand Isle (1965).

The work sheets are not intended to take care of all the features of American English, whether phonological, grammatical or lexical. The purpose of a linguistic atlas is not that of a dictionary or of a full descriptive grammar. Its chief purpose is to determine the dissemination of <u>selected</u> features by areas and by social groups. That some items are included and emphasized does not mean that investigators should not include other items characteristic of their areas or appealing to their special interests. The investigators in Newfoundland and Louisiana have added many fishing terms; in any area, an investigator interested in the vocabulary of a particular group--<u>e.g.</u>, hard-rock miners, oystermen or vineyard workers--can easily explore his special interests by asking additional questions of informants familiar with those occupations. Moreover, as American society becomes increasingly urbanized and the attention of scholars is directed to the language of urban communities, it will be important to follow the precedent of Pederson and explore the vocabulary of urban living. In any event, so long as scholars are working with a living language, they will continue to discover items which deserve investigation; as Gilliéron remarked, one can devise a perfect questionnaire only after all the field work is done.

Nor should an investigator feel that any item is sacrosanct and must be asked regardless of its relevance to his region. What is true is that the work sheets have a core of extremely common words, which provide data on most of the phonological problems of English and a cross-section of grammatical and lexical items with known or suspected regional or social variants. A person basing his investigations on the work sheets can be sure that his data will be comparable with that obtained in other regions, so that he will have the means for ascertaining the relationship of the speech of his region to other forms of American English.

Preface to the Second Edition

The first version of this Compilation was prepared in
a small mimeographed edition in 1951, as a convenience to
American scholars and to those in other lands who were
planning surveys of dialects of English and wished to know
the kinds of questions that had proved useful for providing
comparable data on pronunciation, grammar, vocabulary and
meanings. It was also intended to be a reference work to
indicate to the general linguist the scope of Linguistic
Atlas investigations, the types of data sought, and the
kinds of items used to provide such data. In both of these
roles the compilation was successful.

What was not anticipated, however, was that a revival
of interest in dialect studies would lead to a larger demand
for the compilation both as a reference work and as a text-
book, so that the first edition was rapidly exhausted. By
this time, however, the archives for the Atlantic Seaboard
had been transferred to the University of Chicago. Through
the encouragement of the University of Chicago Press, which
has arranged to publish the Atlas of the Middle and South
Atlantic States, it was decided to issue a new edition of
the compilation, as the first of what promises to be an
extensive series of Chicago publications in American dialec-
tology.

For this edition, the editors have examined not only
the regional questionnaires which were included in the 1951
version but all others based on Linguistic Atlas techniques
that have been used to survey English dialects in the New
World. The contents of all these questionnaires have been
included in the new version, except for the one used in the
Linguistic Atlas of Jamaica by David DeCamp, now of the
University of Texas. Properly keyed to the peculiar ecology
and culture of the West Indies, DeCamp's work sheets diverge
in content very sharply from those used in the United States
and Canada. One suspects that they will be an admirable
model for future investigations of dialects of West Indian
English, and perhaps the nucleus of another compilation.

Besides a few changes in the arrangement of entries,
described below, the most important change from the earlier
version is in the recognition of dialect differences in
urban speech, and in the suggestion of kinds of questions
that will provide information about those differences.
On the one hand this led to expansion of the work sheets
by Lee Pederson, in his study of Chicago speech, with such
additions as parts of an automobile, cuts of meat, and
children's games; on the other, to the sharply curtailed
work sheets for the study of social dialects in Chicago--a
version restricted largely to problems of pronunciation and
a few of the most significant grammatical features.

The work sheets, it is conceded, still have relatively
few syntactic items, in comparison with those dealing
with pronunciation, inflections and vocabulary. The
reason is simple: the more complicated the item, the more
difficult it is to frame questions to elicit, unequivocably,
specific natural responses. Syntactic items are best
recorded in free conversation. Similarly, the supraseg-
mentals--stress, intonation and juncture--are very difficult
to study by direct questioning, since directed responses
in this aspect of language are easily subject to distortion.
One may make the same observation about the complex of
features that are labeled <u>paralanguage</u>: drawl, clipping,
rasp, openness and various modifications of rhythm, pitch
and intensity. For these one needs at least complete
sentences, and preferably passages of connected discourse,
which are almost impossible to record at one fell swoop by
the methods of impressionistic transcription in the field,
but which can easily be preserved on tapes, for repeated
examination.

In fact, one might say that the greatest difference
between field work today and prior to 1951 lies in the fact
that one now has the tape recorder; it can record on the
spot a far more complete record of a speaker's usage than
the most expert field phonetician. It can pick up more of
his unguarded responses; and its record can be reëxamined,
repeatedly, for phonetic detail.

But the virtues of the tape recorder can themselves be
limitations. The unaided field phonetician knows that he
must ask the questions to elicit the responses; that if one
frame of questioning fails to elicit the responses, he
must shift to another, and that if the informant in unguarded
conversation uses a form different from his guarded usage,
it must be recorded on the spot or lost forever. Some
of the earliest field records made with the assistance of
the tape recorder were disappointing in that the investigators did not ask the proper questions to get the responses
and somehow provided far less grammatical evidence, even
for principal parts of common verbs, than the records made
by unaided field transcription.

It is idle to lament that we no longer have field
workers who can transcribe detailed impressionistic phonetics
with speed and accuracy like Guy S. Lowman, Jr., and
Bernard Bloch. We should no more deplore the tape recorder
than the camera or the typewriter. But with all such
mechanical aids we should realize that they are mindless
servants, incapable of acting on their own. They are no
better than the scholar who uses them.

To make the best use of the tape recorder in connection with these work sheets, or with any similar instrument for eliciting dialect information, the field worker should bear a few things in mind throughout the interview.

1) He should be sure that questions are asked that elicit, insofar as the topics are relevant to the local culture, all the desired responses. If he does not try to transcribe simultaneously, he must make notations on some sort of scoring sheet.

2) Better yet, even if he is unable to get exhaustive phonetic detail, he should transcribe as much as possible during the interview without interrupting the flow of discourse. It is far easier to fill in the details of a broad transcription than to take all the evidence off cold tape. Besides, even the best recorder sometimes fails to work, and some informants who will accept the field worker's notebook will balk at mechanical recordings.

3) In listening to the tapes of interviews, the investigators should examine carefully the undirected statements of the informant, including anecdotes and casual remarks. Such spontaneous utterances provide valuable evidence on an informant's natural usage, especially in matters of grammar.

4) In conducting the interview, the investigator should not assume that the tape recorder makes it possible to shorten materially the time for an interview. If the interviewer tries conscientiously to get responses--and if he does not try, he vitiates the purpose of the interview--it is doubtful if he could work faster than the interviewers who have proceeded in the traditional manner; some of them have completed the long work sheets in as little as four hours, the short one in two. Moreover, the very anecdotes which slow up the interview provide evidence not only on conversational usage of items in the work sheets, but also on syntax and suprasegmentals and paralanguage, to say nothing of local history and folklore. In short, the field worker must always use the work sheets in a situation which approximates as closely as possible everyday conversation between two people interested in a common topic.

Virginia McDavid
Raven I. McDavid, Jr.
Alva L. Davis

Arrangement of the Work Sheets

This compilation is paginated, basically, like the work sheets for New England, as printed in the New England *Handbook*, with two exceptions (1) for the basic compilation, pages 1, 55 and 60 are subdivided, giving 1-1A, 55-55A, 60-60A, and pages 7A and 104 are added, as in the work sheets for the Middle and South Atlantic States; (2) for the supplementary materials pages 105-106 are added, as in the preliminary form of the Southern work sheets. Since the pagination of the short work sheets varies considerably from one regional or local survey to another, no attempt has been made to supply it.

Each page has been divided into two parts. The first part includes the items for the work sheets composed by Kurath and his successors.

Unmarked	Items investigated throughout the Atlantic Seaboard
N	Linguistic Atlas of New England
M	Middle Atlantic work sheets
S	South Atlantic work sheets
#	Generalized short work sheets
e	Reduced work sheets for Southern England
c	Abridged work sheets for Chicago social dialect survey
+	Items restored to the short work sheets in three or more regional and local surveys (If restored once or twice, the surveys are specified)

***

The second part of each page, set off from the first part by asterisks, includes items <u>not</u> regularly investigated in any part of the Atlantic Seaboard:

N	Preliminary New England work sheets
S	Preliminary Southern work sheets
L	Linguistic Survey of Louisiana
l	Vocabulary Study of Lafourche Parish and Grand Isle, Louisiana

G	Linguistic Atlas of the North-Central States (=Great Lakes Region)
U	Linguistic Atlas of the Upper Midwest
o	Linguistic Atlas of Oklahoma
R	Linguistic Atlas of the Rocky Mountain States
T	Linguistic Survey of Texas
t	Survey of the Speech of Terre Haute, Indiana
m	Linguistic Atlas of the Maritimes
n	Linguistic Atlas of Newfoundland
P	Linguistic Atlas of the Pacific Coast States
C	Linguistic Survey of Chicago

Individual items are not numbered, but appear in the sequence in which they occur in the work sheets. If the position of an item varies from one survey to another, it appears in its position in the work sheets for the Middle and South Atlantic States. The subdivisions of items reflect the practice of the field workers in interviewing.

The parts of phrases printed in parentheses are included to establish the context in which the item should normally be obtained; they are not necessarily recorded by the field workers.

Phrases between slanting lines / / are directions for the field worker.

Words or phrases following an asterisk are known regional or social variants (the editors of local surveys have not always indicated such variants). In this compilation, the directions for the field worker and the lists of variants have been considerably expanded, though without any pretense at being exhaustive. No matter how many records a field worker has made, he should always be prepared for new variants.

Items listed without variants or directions to the field worker, such as numerals and place names, are included for pronunciation. Underscored words and phrases are also included for pronunciation, and should be recorded if current. To elicit them it is sometimes necessary to alter the context. Thus a field worker seeking the pronunciation of tube may find that some informants know little about the inner tube of an automobile tire but are thoroughly familiar with the priming tube of a muzzle loading gun, or with tube as a container for toothpaste or shaving cream.

3

MS		Do you say 'good night' in meeting?
#		we start to work before) sunrise *sunup
# e		the sun) rose (at six /when did the sun rise?/ *riz, raised, came up
#		we work until) sunset *sundown
# e c		yesterday
l o		he came) Sunday a week /record equivalents/
l o		is he coming) Sunday a week? /record equivalents/
S +		fortnight

***

NL   he came) after <u>dark</u> /in the evening/ *afternight, after dusk, after sundown, after sunset, after supper

L   it's getting) <u>dark</u>

N   he did it <u>last</u> night   *done

4

e c   <u>tomorrow</u>

m o   what time is it?   *what time have you? what time are you? what o'clock is it?

e   a gold) <u>watch</u>

e c   <u>half</u> past seven /7:30/   *after seven

e   <u>quarter</u> of eleven /10:45/   *to, till

N m o   for quite) a while   *a spell

e c   <u>this year</u>

```
                        ***

        c     this-here

SL            stay a spell    *stay a while

SL            he spelled me (off  /temporarily replaced me/

  L           we work from) can to can't   *kin to can't,
                 can't to can't

        1     I'll be there) at eight o'clock   *for eight
                 o'clock


                         5

              he is) three year(s) old

  # e         a year ago

        o     it's a) nice day   *pretty, fine

N       m     it's a) gloomy day  *smurry, dreary, glummerin',
                 lowery

  # e         it's a) clearing, fairing up, fairing off

        m     the weather is) changing  /when rain or snow
                 is expected/  *breaking, gathering, turning,
                 threatening (a storm)

S             clouds

                        ***

N             for four year(s)

SL            he's going to be (ten   *going on, coming;
                 he'll make ten in (June

SL            he's) up in eighty   *over eighty

SL            it's) hazy   *smoky

T       o     clouds are) gathering   *making up

N             the sun is) hidden   *hid
```

```
  +        heavy rain   /of short duration/   *duck
           or goose drownder, cloudburst, down-pour,
           down-fall, squall, gully-washer, trash-
           mover, down-spout, toad-strangler, lightwood-
           knot-floater

# e        thunder storm   *thunder shower, tempest,
           storm, electric(al) storm

#          it) blew (and blew   *blowed

    o      the wind's) from the south   *to the south(w)ard

           a southwest wind; southeast wind   *sou(th)wester,
           sou(th)easter; nor(th)easter, nor(th)wester

           northwest; northeast

MS         a steady drizzle /light fall of rain; short
           or long duration?/   *sprinkle, shower

 N         it's) drizzling   *splitting, spitting

# e        fog

# e        foggy

                        ***

    n      liner /a fall equinoctial storm/   *sneezer,
           auction gale

    n      vapor /moisture arising from fresh or salt
           water after a cold night/   *steam

    l      hurricane /a tropical storm with very high
           winds/   *oragon

    l      oragon /summer storms with wind and rain/
           *squall, a blow

    l      /the weather which precedes a hurricane/
           *squall

    m      /the paper predicts rain/   *wants
```

```
RT    o     /kinds of windstorms/
N     1     cyclone  /a storm with circularly blowing
            winds/   *twister, tornado
T     o     norther  /cold wind with sharply falling
            temperature/   *blue norther, wet norther

N           thunder head   *nigger head

N           it didn't rain a) drop

SL          it's burned off   /only of fog?/   *cleared
            off, cleared away, lifted

      t     it's cooled off  /after a heat wave/   *cooled
            down

      t     the rain has slacked off   *let up

      o     it came up rain
```

7

```
  # e       drought  /long or short?/   *drouth,
            dry spell

  #         the wind is) picking up   *breezing on,
            breezing up fresh, getting stronger,
            rising, raising, gusting, coming up,
            blowing higher

  #         it's) letting up  /strong wind? light wind?/
            *laying, going down, dying down, easing up,
            lulling,abating

N     m     it's) rather snappy (this morning   *sharp,
            edgy, keen, fresh, airish

  # e       we had a) frost  /light or severe?/   *a
            freeze

  # e       the lake) froze over (last night  /thick
            ice or thin? entire surface or just around
            edges?/   *friz, skimmed, skum(med),
            scaled over

  # e       sitting room  /where guests are entertained/
            *big house, parlor, front room, living
            room, best room, hall, keeping room

    m o     the room is) nine foot high   *feet, foots
```

***

n   conkerballs /long slivers of ice hanging
       down from roof of house/ *ice candles

n   ballycatters /ice on shore or rocks from
       waves and salt spray/

n   glitter /ice formed on trees, bushes and
       wires from freezing rain/ *silver thaw

n   squall /sudden snow-storm/   *dwye

n   Sheil(y)a's brush /a snowfall about 17-
       20 March/

n   clumper /small floating iceberg/   *clamper,
       growler

SL   m   it's) frozen (solid   *froze, friz

URP   scum /first thin coating of ice/   *shale
             ice, anchor ice, mush ice, skim, skift, scum

RT   /kinds of snow storms/ *blizzard, norther

RP   /warm wind in winter; moist or dry? get
             direction/   *chinook, thaw

7A

MS   +   Make a floor plan of the house and name the
             rooms

```
N    #   c    chimney  /on house/    *flue
         m    chimney  /of an industrial plant; on
                  a ship/   *smoke stack, funnel

     # e      hearth  /on fireplace? raised shelf on
                  stove?/   *hearthstone

     #        the lamp, etc., is on the) mantle shelf
                  /always over fireplace?/   *mantle piece,
                  mantle, tussock, clock shelf, fire board,
                  mantle board, mantle tree

     #        back log   *log, back-stick, chunk

S    +        lightwood  /fatty kindling sticks/   *lighterd,
                  pine, kindling, fat-wood

MU            burn coal) in (the stove   *into

     # e c    soot  /ever pl.?/

MS # e c      it burns to) white ashes   *a white ash
              the ashes are (white   *is

     # e c    chair

                         ***

SL            picture

         n    stove  /types/
         m    fender  /around fireplace/   *firescreen

SL            chunk  /split wood for stove/  *billet,
                  stick
         n    splints  /small slivers of wood to start fire/
                  *bavins

         n    junk  /sizes of wood burned/

U             kitchen matches  /will strike on any surface/
                  *parlor matches, farm(ers) matches

L    c        window

C             /kinds of heating units and methods of circu-
                  lation/

C             water heater  /describe/
         l    /ashes in a fireplace banked for the night/
         o    fire
```

```
   # e     sofa  /describe!/   *lounge, couch, chester-
                field, davenport, daybed

      +     chest of drawers  /describe!/   *dresser,
                bureau, chiffonier, chifferobe

N       o   What is a 'bureau'?  /record pronunciation/

MS     +    furniture   *house fixings, plunder, tricks
                /downstairs? upstairs?/

N  # e      bedroom   *chamber, sleeping house
M           bedsink  /alcove containing bed/   *sink
                bedroom

   #        window shades  /roller shades/   *blinds,
                curtains

   #        clothes closet  /built in/   *clothes press,
                closet, press, wardrobe

MS     +    wardrobe  /movable; any difference between
                tall massive antique and lighter modern
                pieces?/   *wardroom, clothes press, press,
                armoire

   # e      garret   *attic, sky parlor, cock loft

   # e      kitchen  /describe; winter or summer kitchen?/
                *porch, cook house, cook room, stove room,
                kitchen house

                       ***

T          hatrack   *clothes tree

P          suite of furniture

L          piano

T          lamp) cord

SL C       summer kitchen  *cellar kitchen
   C           /bathroom and equipment/

     1     dressing table  /a small low table with mirror
                and usually with drawers on each side/
                *dresser, vanity
```

```
       1     safe  /piece of kitchen furniture for
                   keeping food, dishes, etc./   *kitchen
                   cabinet

C                  /types of apartment buildings/   *two flat,
                   three flat

       o     mirror


                           10

    #  e     pantry    *buttery, kitchen closet, safe

       +     junk  /old, worthless furniture and implements/
                   *cultch, rubbish, trash, plunder, trumpery

N  #         she cleans up (every morning   *tidies (up),
                   reds (up), rids (up)

    #  e     the broom is behind (the door   *in back of,
                   tohind, hindside, back of

    #  c     who does the) washing and ironing   *laundry
                   laundry  /commercial/

N      c     I rented a room   *hired

NC           apartment   *tenement, flat  /distinguish
                   between flat and apartment/

MS   m o     stairway   *stairsteps, stairs, staircase

    # e c    porch  /at front door; at back door; describe
                   construction/   *gallery, veranda, piazza,
                   balcony, stoop, breezeway, dog trot, dog run

MU           file cloth  /damp cloth for wiping floor; with
                   sand?/
MU           file (the floor

                          ***

RP           cellar  /describe/   *basement

MP           cellar porch   *cellar entrance

       n     back-porch  /small room added to back of house/

P      1     flat iron  /not electric/   *sad iron,
                   smoothing iron

       o     storm cellar
```

```
      #    c    shut the door     *close, pull the door to

 N               who) rang (the bell?     *rung

         +       weatherboards     *clapboards, siding, weather
                   boarding, sheathing, facerboards

     #  e  c     I drove in (a nail     *druv, driv

 MS  #  e        the posts have to be) driven in     *druv

  N  #  e        I have driven (many a nail     *druv

     #     c     roof

     #  e        eaves troughs   /built in or suspended?/
                   *gutters, spouting, canals, canales, rain
                   gutters, drain pipes

        m  o     valley   /of joining roofs/     *gutter, alley

 NM  #           shed   /for wood, tools, etc.; separate and
                   built on/    *ell, hill house, lean-to, wood-
                   house, woodshed, cob house, tool house,
                   tool shed

                        ***

         m       downspout   /carrying water from eavestroughs
                   to drain/

 TP              shakes   /boards split or riven as a substitute
                   for shingles/    *clapboards

 RTP     o       adobe   /sun-dried clay for building/    *dobe
 RP              adobes   /earth blocks used in building; mixed
                   with straw?/    *sod blocks, terrones

 RP              beams   /roof supports/    *joists, rafters, vigas

 R               root cellar   *root house, potato pit, potato
                   cellar, potato cave, potato dugout

 RP              yard   /describe/    *court, patio
  P              covered walk   *arcade, breezeway, galery
  P              they will) tint the walls   /interior only?/
                   *paint
         l       house that is finished with plaster on the
                   outside   (stucco)
         l       shotgun house   /a long house one room wide,
                   of two or three rooms/
```

```
   +          out-house   /separate structure; usual word;
                 jocular words/   *back-house, toilet,
                 privy, necessary, outdoors, garden house,
                 biffy, commode, cabine

         o    I have my (troubles    *I've got
                 you ...
                 we ...

  # e c      I have heard it (lots of times  /unstressed 'have'/
  N          he ...
  N          they ...
  MS         I've) heard (of him    *heerd tell

  #   c      I haven't (seen him  /unstressed/   *ain't
             he ...

  # e c      I haven't   /stressed, in answer to 'Have you
                 seen him?'/   *hain't, ain't
             he ...

  S     o    you are going,) enty?  /is 'enty' used for all
                 persons, sing. and pl.?/   *ain't

    m o      I do it (all the time
             he ...
             we ...

      m      does he do (that sort of thing?   *do he do

  #   c      he does  /stressed/   *do, dooz

                      ***

  SL         you) ain't (forget it, enty?  /stress and
                 intonation/   *haven't forgotten
```

13

```
# e        he doesn't care    *don't

S          you don't think so,) do you?    *enty

S          don't I know it?    *ain't I knows it?

N          I work (all day
           we work ...
           they ...

MS         I'm not for sure    *sure

     m     I was talking (to him
     m     you ...
N          we ...
N          they ...

  #        I have been thinking (about it
N          we ...
N          they ...

ST   o     what) make (him do it   /enter other cases of
              the uninflected 3 sing./

     m     people think(s) (he did it

     m     they say (he did it    *says

                     ***

L          since) I am here those five years   /is the
              present tense used in expressions of time
              where English normally has the perfect?/
              *since) I've been here


                     14

N          says I, ('you can't fool me!'   /=I said';
              form in which quotations introduced in
              narratives/    *I says

           says you, ...    *you says
           says we, ...    *we says
           says they, ...    *they says

MS #       house; houses

  # e      barn /what used for?   take down all compounds/
```

```
      # e        corn crib   /building for storing corn/
                    *corn barn, corn house, crib

N     # e        granary   /building, or part of building, for
                    storing grain/

L     # e        loft   /upper part of barn; describe or
                    make sketch/   *barn chamber, mow,
                    scaffold, overhead, great-beams

      #          hay stack   /observe shape and size; out of
                    of doors or in barn?/   *rick, mow

M                hay barrack   /four poles and sliding roof/
                    *rick, haystack, hay cap, Dutch cap

MS  # e          cock   /in field at haying time/   *tumble,
                    haycock, doodle, shock, heap, pile, coil,
                    rick, mow

NM  #            /places for hay in barn; describe/   *loft,
                    bay, mow

                            ***

        m        /first heap of hay raked up after windrow/
        m        /second heap of hay raked up or piled/

        l        /main plantation house/

P       l        yard   /area surrounding a house in town/
                    *garden, lot
SL               bank barn    *ground barn

R     o          silo   /pit? trench? building?/   *pit silo,
                    trench silo

SL               a place) for keep (corn   *for keeping

 L               to) shuck fodder   /strip blades off corn
                    stalks/   *pull fodder

N                two rick(s) of hay   /define 'rick'/

P                farm   /small country place where crops are
                    grown/   *ranch

        t        tarpaulin   *canvas

        o        /name of early settlers house type/   *sod,
                    dugout, etc.
```

15

```
# e       cow barn  /shelter for cows; describe!/
          *barn, stable, cow shed, lean-to, tie-up,
          linny

N      m  stable  /shelter for horses; describe!/
          *barn

S      o  milk gap  /place where cows are 'staked'
          or 'penned' for milking; describe!/
          *cow pen, cuppin

  #       hog pen  /shelter and enclosure for hogs
          and pigs; describe!/  *hog run, hog crawl,
          sty, hog boist, hog house, pig pen

# e o     dairy  /place for milk and butter?  type of
          farm?/

# e       barnyard  /where stock is kept or fed/  *stable
          lot, cow lot, sheep lot, horse lot, pightle,
          corral

# e       pasture  /where cows, sheep, etc. graze/
          *lot, range
```

***

```
S         stanchions   *stanchels

N         bee hive   *bee gum, gum

S         barn lot  /for thrashing, etc.; not for
          stock/   *lot, yard

R         corral  /near barn or in field?  size?  struc-
          ture?  purpose?/  *barnyard, barn lot,
          feed lot, park, back yard, stockade, night
          yard

       n  garden  /enclosed area for grass, hay/

       c  dairy  /is milk company the primary meaning?/
```

16

```
       o  field  /size and purpose; does term vary with
          crop?/  *patch, lot, a piece of (tobacco, etc.

  #       picket fence  /woven or nailed?/  *paling
          fence, pale fence, slat fence, garden,
          shingle garden
```

N   m o   pickets /pointed or not? shape in cross-
                        section/   *palings, slats

   #   barb(ed) wire fence   *bob-wire fence

   #   rail fence /describe construction! is
                        there more than one type?/ *worm fence,
                        herring bone fence, Virginia fence, chain
                        fence, snake fence, stake and rider fence,
                        shad fence, galloping fence, rip-gut (fence)

   # e   post(e)s /the plural/

   #   stone wall /of loose stones/   *stone fence,
                        rock fence, rock wall

N   tin cup /with small looped handle or
                        straight handle/   *tin, dipper, mug, tin
                        jug, tin can, gourd

                             ***

L   o   to chop cotton /weed a cotton field with a
                        hoe/   *scrape cotton
      o   to pick cotton

L   cocoa grass /undesirable grass in cotton
                        field or other planted land; get different
                        kinds/   *nut grass, johnson grass, Bermuda
                        grass, wire grass, crawling grass,
                        alligator grass

L   palings /thin strips, split or riven out
                        for fencing, roofing, etc./   *clapboards,
                        slats

L   to rive (palings /get principal parts if
                        possible/   *split palings

L   froe /instrument for splitting palings/

L   to) wattle (palings into a fence   *weave

L   stringers /cross pieces through which fence
                        palings are woven or wattled/

L   yard fence /front yard? back yard? different
                        types/

L   fencing /degree of obstruction/

       n   /other kinds of fences/   *riddlin-rod fence,
                        link fence, stump fence

C   steel fence /metal mesh fence enclosing
a playground, factory, military installa-
tion, etc./   *cyclone fence

    o   stake *stob

  l o   staple /u-shaped nail to attach wire to
posts/ *steeple

    t   /other -sts forms/ *tests, guests,
communists, scientists

17

\# e c   <u>china</u> /record also <u>china</u> egg/ *delft(ware)

\# e   bucket /wooden vessel; shape and use;
get compounds/ *pail, piggin

\# e   pail /large open tin vessel for water,
milk/ *bucket

NP   l   lunch pail /small tin vessel with cover
for carrying dinner/ *bucket, billy,
blick, box, dinner bucket

  \#   garbage pail /describe!/ *garbage can,
swill bucket, ort pail, swill pail,
slop pail, slop bucket

\# e   fry(ing) pan /flat or round bottom?
iron or sheet metal? legs?/ *skillet,
spider, creeper

\# e   <u>kettle</u> /heavy iron vessel with large opening;
shape; get meaning of kettle/ *pot,
caldron, (wash) boiler

MS \#   vase *flower(s) pot

MS \#   <u>spoon</u>

***

  m   waste /unwanted food/ *scraps, orts, garbage

  m   skillet /to boil water on hearth/ *saucepan

  n   skim /stick used for stirring porridge
or mixing cakes; for cooking fish in big
pot; for stirring oil/

C   hand towel   *face towel

C   garbage can /large galvanized refuse can/
              *trash can, ash can, GI can

C   electric frying pan   *skillet

C   /permanent refuse constructions serviced
            by local garbage collectors/

C   /what does <u>garbage</u> mean?/

    1   wash boiler /utensil used to boil clothes in/

    1   wash tub /galvanized tub used for washing
          clothes or for bathing/   *No. 3 tub

18

\# e c   I must) <u>wash</u> the dishes

\# e c   she) <u>rinses</u> (the dishes

   +   dish rag /for washing dishes/

\#   dish towel /for wiping dishes/ *dish wiper,
       tea towel, dry-rag, cup towel

N   +   wash cloth /for face/ *face cloth, wash rag

\# e   bath <u>towel</u> *Turkish towel

\# e c   faucet /on water pipe at kitchen sink; in
       yard; on barrel/ *tap, spigot, spicket,
       hydrant, cock

   o   the pipe) burst (last night

N		they must have) burst (last night
N		an <u>empty</u> glass
N		sifter /for sifting flour/ *sieve
MS	#	<u>barrel</u> /for meal, flour/ *gum
MS		stand /for molasses, lard/
	#	funnel *tunnel
	# e c	<u>whip</u> /for driving horses/
	# e	goad /for oxen/ *lash
N		switch /for punishing children/ *gad, hickory, rattan, ferule, shillelagh
	# e c	paper bag /made of paper; size/ *bag, poke, meal sack
MS	# e	burlap bag *sack, gunny sack, crocus sack, tow sack, guano sack, coffee sack
MS	#	turn (of corn, meal, wood, water, etc. /the quantity of corn taken to the mill at one time; a load on the back; a load (of wood) in arms; a part load/ *load, chance, jag, grist(e), armful, arm load

***

TP		<u>tin</u> <u>can</u>
P		<u>bottle</u>
T		olla /large jar for drinking water/ *water jug
N		sieve /for sifting gravel/ *sifter
SL		Are 'poke', 'sack', etc. used as measures? Is 'a turn of meal (flour)' used as 'a turn of corn'?
	n	/half barrel/
	n	puncheon /large cask, 72-gal./ *puncheon tub
	n	yaffle /arm load of fish; small pile/

C   shopping bag /describe/

C   cleaning bag   *plastic bag

C   bag attached to electric sweeper

     o   light bulb

C   vacuum cleaner

              20

  # e   clothes basket

  #   keg /small barrel: for whisky? for nails?
            to plant cod trap?/   *kag

  # e   hoops

  # e   cork /for bottle; material? glass? cork?
            rubber?/   *cork stopple, stopple, stopper

     +   mouth organ   *harp, harmonica, mouth harp,
            French harp

  # e   hammer

  # e   tongue /of a wagon/   *heap, pole, spear

  # e   shafts /of a buggy/   *shavs, thills, fills,
            drafts

              ***

N   pen holder   *pen staff

GURT PCo   Jew's harp /held between teeth and plucked/
           *juice harp, jaws harp

C   clothes hamper /describe/

C   bottle cap

     o   mallet   *maul

```
    m o     steel) rim  /of wheel/   *tire
      o     felly  /of wood/

  # e     whiffletree   *whippletree, swingletree,
            singletree

  #       evener   *doubletree, spreader, double singletree

  # e     he was) hauling (wood in his wagon   *drawing,
            carting

      o     dragged (a log, etc.   *drug

  # e     plow

  # e     harrow  /describe; type?/   *drag

NM #      stone boat  /for transporting stones from
            field; no wheels/   *drag, mud boat,
            stone gear, stone slip, skerry

                    ***

SL        axle   *ex
    m     he was) hauling logs   *snirging

L         gee-whiz   *spring-tooth harrow

N         plow  /for cultivating/   *cultivator

UR  m     go-devil  /triangular frame for hauling supplies?
            for cultivating corn?  for digging or cleaning
            ditches?  for cleaning pipelines?  for
            chiseling hard soil?  one-horse disk plow?
            sled cultivator, as for frijoles?  low-slung
            sled for high-speed coasting?  other meanings?/
            *go-dig, travois, try-boy, draw-boy

C         /small clawed tool for breaking dirt in garden;
            describe or sketch/

C         rake  /distinguish lawn, garden; metal or
            wooden tines/

C         lawn mower  /manual/
C         lawn mower  /power/

C         roller coaster  /transcribe several types of
            fast-moving amusement park rides on rails/
```

N   <u>lever</u>   /of steel or iron/   *prize, crowbar

   # e c   saw-buck   /for sawing firewood?   planks?/
              *saw-horse, trestle, saw-jack

N   <u>cog</u> wheel

   # e c   <u>brush</u>   *bresh

   # e   <u>strop</u>   /for sharpening razor/

   # e   <u>cartridge</u>

   # e   seesaw   *teetering board, teeter-totter, dandle,
             tilt(s), ridy-horse, hicky-horse, cock-horse,
             teeter-horse, see-horse, tiltamo, way-de-
             buckety

S   +   joggling board   /limber plank suspended at both
             ends/
S   +   flying jenny   /home-made-merry-go-round/
             *flying Dutchman, whirligig, ridy-horse

MS   m   they are) seesawing   *teetering, tilting

NM #   sled   / for boys; describe the various types
             used/   *bob-sled, cutter, double runner,
             double ripper, roller-coaster, pung, slide

***

N   <u>strap</u>   /to put around trunk/

R   guns   /different types and purposes; ordinary
             names and pet names/   *forty rod, shooting
             iron, lightning rod

PT   l o   slingshot   /boy's weapon made of forked stick
             with rubber strips/   *beanie, nigger-
             shooter, catapult

SLP   n   swing   /board suspended by rope from a limb
             or bar/   *swing-swang

      m   <u>toboggan</u>

      n   sled   /for general hauling/

      n   sled   /for hauling salt or fish; box or flat
             platform on runners/

```
     n      catamaran   /for hauling logs in the woods
                on snow:  box or flat platform on runners/
             *dog-cat

     m      stage coach    *stage

     c      candle

     c      (railroad) trestle

     t      dynamite
```

                              23

```
# e      coal hod    *scuttle

         stovepipe    *funnel

# e      wheelbarrow    *trucks

# e      whetstone  /for sharpening scythe/    *whetrock,
            rifle, rubstone

# e      grindstone    *grinston

         can you drive a) car?    *auto(mobile),
            motor car

N        he pleaded (guilty    *plead

# e c    grease (the car

# e c    greasy
```

                              ***

```
NP       nut  /on bolt/    *tap

TP       a) brand new car

S        he) greased (it    *grez
C        the car needs) a grease job    *a lube job,
            a greasing

C        accelerator  /on car floor?  on dash?/   *gas

C        /auto instrument panel/    *dashboard, dash, panel

C        /small compartment on dash/    *glove compartment

C        /automobiles with two doors/
```

C   /automobiles with more than two doors/
                   *four door, wagon, station wagon

C   /vehicles used for milk, pizza, cleaning and
                   parcel delivery; distinctions?/

24

\# e c   <u>oil</u>

MS   + c   kerosene   *coal oil, lamp oil, carbon oil,
                   stove oil

\#   c   inner) <u>tube</u>

\# e   they are going) to <u>launch</u> the boat
N   m   a launch /a boat <u>pointed</u> at both ends?
                   rectangular? flatbottomed? used for hunting
                   or fishing?/

MS   +   rowboat   *bateau, john boat, pirogue

\# e c   I am going (today /is auxiliary verb omitted?/
                   we ...
N   they ...

\# e c   am I going (to get some?
                   ... they ...

***

N   o   these are (the kind I like /e.g., cigars,
                   apples/   *them's

L   <u>park</u> (the car

L   <u>gas</u>   *gasoline

L   <u>gallon</u>

L   we (are) good /is 'be' omitted with predicate
                   adjectives?/

L   we going to town /is the auxiliary 'be' omitted?/
                   *we are going

       m   lantern /hand carried/

       m   lamp   /on boat/

      m n   /types of boats: how propelled? size? rigging?/
                   *rodney, punt, collar boat, long liner, flat,
                   western boat, schooner, dory, skiff, gondola,
                   dinghy

25

```
# e        here are your clothes!  /mother to child/
               *here's

      o    there are (many people that think so   *there's

# e c      I am not (going to hurt him   *ain't
N          he ...
N          they ...

# e c      I'm right,) am I not?   *ain't I

# e c      we were (going to do it anyway   *was
N     o    you ...
N     o    they ...

N          those were (the good old days   *them was

# e c      no, it wasn't me   *wan't

                    ***

L          there are) right smart (of them   *many
L          there are plenty of 'em   *enough
      o    there were (lots of 'em   *there was

N          you're not old enough,) are you?   *is, air
```

26

```
N # e      be you going?  /enter phrases like 'how be you,'
               'he's busier than I be'/

N          if I were you, (I wouldn't wait a minute
               longer  /intonation!/   *was

           sample  /of cloth/

N     o    that's a) pretty (dress

      o    she has a) prettier (dress   *more prettier

  #        apron  /describe different kinds/   *smock

                    ***

TP         button

TP    o    hem

NL         I saw the) prettiest (dress!   *best
```

TP   o   <u>safety</u> <u>pin</u>

       m   apron /for children/   *tyer, pinafore,
                 pinny

SL   underwear   *undershifts

P   head scarf /tied under chin/   *kerchief,
                 fascinator, babushka, tiyon, tyer

27

   # e   <u>coat</u>
M   +   the coat has buttons) on (it   *onto

MS # e   vest   *jacket, weskit

MS # e   trousers /material? for dress? for work?/
              *pants, breeches, jeans

   # e c   I have) brought (your coat   *brung

   # e   his coat) fitted (me   *fit

   # e   <u>new</u> <u>suit</u>

   # e c   the pockets) <u>bulge</u>

NP   they) knitted (sweaters for the soldiers
            *knit

    +   the collar) shrank   *shrunk, drawed up

N   +   it has shrunk   *shrunken

M   m   winklehawk /three-cornered tear in coat or
            pants/   *rinklehawk, nagelloch

***

    n   <u>scissors</u>

    t   car coat /less than full-length outer coat/
            *finger-tip, three quarter, suburban

C   shorts /knee length outer garments; distinguish
         men and women/

SLR   l   overalls   *denims, jeans, blue bucks,
                  levis, overhauls

       l   /the zippered opening on a pair of pants/

RT   o   <u>chaps</u> /leather leggings reaching to waist
                  for riding, especially in brush/

SL   I) got me (a new suit   *myself
SL   I) had me (a new suit   *myself

       m   buttons

L   it'll <u>shrink</u>

       t   <u>collar</u>

```
        o      she likes to) dress up    *dike up, rig up,
                  slick up, prink up, primp up, doll up, dike out

  # e c    purse  /for coins/   *pocket book

  # e      bracelet

MS    o    string of beads    *pair of beads

N          half-shoes   *low(-cut) shoes, oxfords, ties,
             low-quarters, slippers

      o    suspenders   *galluses, braces

  # e c    an old) umbrella

  # e      bed-spread   *coverlet, coverlid, counterpane

MS    o    pillow   *piller

MS         bolster

MS    + c  it goes) clear (across   *clean, plum, slam
             jam
```

                                    ***

```
      m    cuffs  /wool/   *wristbands, wristlets,
             rizbans, stub rubbers

L          wallet  /for bills/   *pocketbook, bill fold

NP         rubbers  /not covering the ankles/   *gum shoes,
             over-shoes

STP  l o   pillow slip   *pillowcase, pillow bier, pillow
             cover

      l    tester  /canopy over a bed/   *teester

      l    /long stick used in making beds and in
             smoothing bed clothing/

      l    mosquito bar  /fine thin cloth that lets air
             in and keeps mosquitoes and other insects
             out/   *bar, baire
```

```
    # e        quilt  /washable, tied/   *comforter, comfort,
                   comfortable, puff, soogan

MS  # e        pallet  /bed on floor/   *shakedown, lodge

 N             fertile

     +         bottom land  /flat low-lying land along a
                   stream; flooded in spring, plowed later/
                   *low-land, intervale, flat(s), bottom(s),
                   batture

    # e        meadow  /low-lying grass land/   *swale,
                   bayou (land), mash land, prairie, dago

    # e        swamp  /inland; open or overgrown; may it have
                   trees?/   *slough, marsh, bog, gall, cienega,
                   sinigie, mud flats, mish, mash

    # e        marshes  /along the sea/   *salt marshes

MN  # e        loam  /poor soil; sandy/   *loom, buckshot(land)
               muck  /rich soil; black/   *loom, loam, gumbo

                        ***

UP             quilt  /quilted/   *comforter, comfort, soogan

         n     blanket  /woolen covering for bed/   *rug

N              soil  /define variants/   *dirt, earth, ground

RTP      o     flat  /on mountain? in plains? fertile or
                   barren?/   *mesa, prairie

NTP            badlands  /unfit for cultivation/   *malpais,
                   alkali flats, poverty flats, waste land,
                   filth land, barrens

RP             park  /enclosed high altitude basin? any enclosed
                   grassy space?/   *valley, basin, hole

TP   l o       prairie  /flat grassy country/   *plains, flats,
                   llano

U              to) meadow (cows  /to put cows to pasture;
                   get verb!/   *pasture

S              pocosin  /depression formed by meteor/   *bay

T        o     tank  /artificial pool or pond to water live-
                   stock or provide irrigation for rice fields/
                   *reservoir, reserve
```

30

```
      m      they are) draining (the marshes    *dreening

MS m l o     drainage) canal  /sizes/    *drain, cunnel,
               trenance

      e      creek  /shallow arm of the sea; tidal steam
               /natural or man-made?/   *bayou, slue,
               bay, cove, inlet, swash

N     +      ravine  /deep, narrow valley of a small stream/
               *draw, glen, gulch, gully, hollow, canyon,
               wash

MS           gully  /channel cut by erosion in road or
               field/

   # e       creek  /small, fresh-water stream; arrange
               by size/   *stream, brook, run, branch,
               fork, prong, gulf, binnekill, binacle,
               rivulet, riverlet, gutter, kill, bayou, coulee,
               burn

   # e       /names of streams in the neighborhood/

N     +      hill  /small elevation; wooded?  bare?
               arrange by size/   *knob, knoll, butte,
               taunch, nap, hummick

                        ***

RP           canyon  /deeply cut valley or gully; only
               between hills?  narrow?  steep sides?
               with stream?/   *gorge, gulch

RP           gulch  /in hillside?  with stream?  size?
               steep or sloping banks?/   *box canyon,
               draw, arroyo

RTP    o     irrigation ditch   *canal, water ditch, acequia,
               sakey ditch

URTP   o     coulee  /small depression with usually dry
               watercourse; steep or sloping banks?/
               *draw, seep, swale, arroyo, wash

T            /principal rivers in territory, as Rio Grande,
               Pecos, Colorado, Brazos, Trinity, Neches,
               Sabine/
```

U   butte   /define/   *knob

P   we go for a swim to the) beach   *coast,
                 ocean, seashore, seaside, shore

P   seawall /wall extending into the ocean/
                 *breakwater, jetty, sandbar

    n o   drain /by side of road/   *ditch, gutter

    n   gulch /salt water flowing in narrow passage/

    n   gulley /small pond/

C   /names for the Chicago River/

C   _prairie_   *lot, vacant lot, subdivision

    1   stream /sluggish water/   *brook, bayou

    1   levee /embankment of earth, by a river,
                 creek to prevent floods/

    1   crevasse /break in levee/

    1   flottant /soft prairie with water underneath/
                 *quaking prairie, trembling prairie

    1   brulee /open place in swamp, usually resulting
                 from fire/

    1   roseaux /reeds or cane which grow in the
                 marsh/

    1   palmetto /plant with fan-shaped leaves, often
                 used to roof houses/

    1   canebrake /place where bamboo grows thick/

    m   rill /first run-off from field/

```
# e         mountain
M     +     notch  /between mountains/    *clove, pass, gap

            cliff    *clift, rock-cliff

# e         wharf  /where boats stop and upon which
              freight is unloaded/    *landing, pier, dock

            waterfall    *pour-over, a falls

# e c       cement road    *concrete road, hard-road,
              pave, pavement

N           Do you still use the word 'turn-pike' or
              'pike'?
            What does it mean?  Name some pikes.

#           by-way  /outside of town/    *neighborhood
              road, back-road, gravel road, parish road,
              country road, dirt road, lane, by-path

# e         lane  /from public road to house; from barn to
              pasture; across public road/    *driveway,
              gap, avenue, cow pass

M     +     sidewalk    *pavement, banquette

                        ***

R           /particular mountain formations/    *knob,
              peak, ridge, bald, dome, butte, etc.
R           /names of mountains, peaks, ranges, etc. in
              neighborhood/

N           shallows  /in a small stream/    *riffle, slashes,
              rapids, shoals

LUP         black-top  /bituminous/    *tarvia road, tarvy
              road, tarvy, oiled road, pavement, pave

        m   fill  /built-up piece of road, especially across
              a small stream/    *abbateau

UR          barrow pit  /place from which dirt is taken
              for highway fill/    *borrow pit, bar pit,
              grader ditch

T           gap  /place to let cars or trains through a
              fence/
```

```
        m    cow pass    *cattle pass

UP           chuck hole   /depression in road/    *chug
                hole, pot hole, hole

URP          the road was) slippery    *slick

URPC    t    boulevard  /grass strip between sidewalk and
                street; distinct from lawn?/   *grass
                strip, berm, parkway, parking strip, tree
                lawn, tree belt, tree row, terrace

N            stone  /flat; in front of door/   *rock

        m    gut  /abrupt break in coastline or mountain
                ridge/

        n    brandies  /submerged rocks with water breaking
                over them/   *breakers, sunkers

    m n      valley  /place between steep hills; no stream,
                with a stream, wooded, bare/   *droke

        n    cliffs

        n    highroad  /unpaved? paved?/   *highway
        l    to catch a bridge  /meaning?/
        n    lane  /narrow way in town or settlement/
        n    line  /road running across country, connecting
                high-roads/

        n    tote-road  /a road in lumberwoods/
        n    cove  /a way going to wharf or water's edge/

C            sidewalk  /between buildings/   *gangway,
                alley, alleyway, passageway

        l    /location of house between the road and bayou/
                *the house is on the) bayou side

C       l    shoulder  /strip of land between highway and
                ditch/   *side, berm

        l    jar  /culvert or drainpipe in the ground/

C            service plaza  /on toll road/   *oasis, service
                area

C            street  /describe/   *road, avenue, boulevard

C            toll road  /describe/   *tollway, thruway,
                expressway
```

C   parallel parking /describe/   *curb
               parking, diagonal parking

C   center strip (on highway

C   ramp /expressway or tool road exit/
               *cloverleaf, exit

C   underpass   *viaduct

32

\# e   he <u>threw</u> a <u>stone</u> (at the dog *rock,
               dornick, doney, hoonie; throwed, chucked,
               chunked, flung, pitched, heaved, hove

\# e c   he isn't) to home   *at home

\# e c   <u>without</u> (milk

\# e c   <u>with</u> (milk /<u>with</u> followed by a voiced sound/

N   he was sitting right) agin me /=close to me/
               *next to me

   + c   he was coming) <u>toward(s)</u> me

\# e   I ran) across (him /=met him/ *into, on(to),
               afoul of

\# e   we named the child) for him *at, after, from

                     ***

L   he) skipped a rock (on the water *skimmed,
               skum, skipping *skimming

N   come to think) of it   *on it

SL   she's) to the house   *at, in
SL   she's) to the kitchen   *at, in

L   't) isn't (my dog /is 'it' omitted?/
               *'tain't, 'isn't, ain't, it isn't, it
               ain't

     o   <u>through</u>

```
      #    c    dog
MS  # e         call to dog to attack another dog
    # e         call to summon dog
    # e         mongrel  /mixed breed; worthless?/   *cur,
                   cur dog, fiste, scrub, hound dog, pot
                   licker, mutt

    # e c       he was) bitten (by a dog   *bit

    # e         bull   *animal, beast, male, top-cow, cow
                   brute, cow critter, toro, tuppin' ox,
                   seed ox, stock cow  /special words used
                   by farmers?  by women?  in presence of
                   women?/

    # e c       cow

    # e         two) yoke(s) of oxen   *pair

      e         calf
N               female calf   *heifer(-calf)
N               male calf   *calf

    #           Daisy is going) to calve,   *find a calf,
                   come in, freshen, come fresh, drop a calf,
                   spring

                          ***

      t         beagle  /a small hound/   *beetle

SL              /call to dog to lie down/

T               cat

C               /call to summon cat/

C               stray cat

TP              dogie  /motherless calf/   *maverick

      m         /two animals worked together; are different
                   terms used for horses and oxen?/
      m         /four animals worked together/

C               /kinds of cats/
C               /kinds of birds you've owned or seen in the
                   yard/
C               /kinds of fish kept and fed/
C               aquarium  /describe/   *bowl
```

+		stallion *stud, stable horse, top-horse, seed horse, service horse, stock horse /special words used by farmers? by women? in presence of women?/

N e gelding   *gelded horse, horse

 # e c <u>horse</u>

N   Do you use the word 'horse' as a general term for geldings, mares, and stallions?

 # e I have never) ridden (a horse   *rode

 # e c he fell) off (the horse *off of, off'n

MS o he fell) out of (bed   *outen the

 # c <u>horseshoes</u>

MS # e <u>hoofs</u>   *hooves

 # e quoits /a game/ *quates, horseshoes, kites

 # ram   *buck, male sheep   /special words used by farmers? by women? in presence of women?/

***

SL   <u>mare</u>

RTP o bronco /unbroken horse/   *bronc, mustang

RTP o pinto /mottled Indian pony; any color combination? black and white only?/   *paint

RT o remuda /band or herd of saddle horses/ *string, cavvy, caballada, caviard

TP1 o burro /small donkey/   *donkey, jackass, jack

TP <u>rear</u> /of a horse trying to throw the rider; get distinction/   *buck, pitch

UP spook /to shy, of a horse/   *shy, start

  m <u>goat</u>
  n goat collar

  n /shearing terms/

```
 # e     ewe   /other words for sheep?/
N    +   pet lamb  /raised on a bottle?  orphan?
            stunted?/   *cosset, cade, penco, pinco

 # e     wool

 # e     boar   *boar hog, male hog, hog, seed hog,
            breeding hog, stock hog
         /special words used by farmers?  by women?
            in presence of women?/

MS   +   barrow   *barrow hog, stag, rig

N        pig  /how old?/   *suckling pig

N        shote  /weaned pig?  how old?/   *yearling,
            feeding hog

 #       hogs  /male and female?  old and young?/

 # e     bristles

MS # e   tusks   *tushes

 # e     trough:  troughs
                        ***

U        bell wether  /define/
```

```
 #       castrate  /horses, bull calves, boars, cats/
            *alter, change, trim, cut, dress, mark,
            work on

 # e     bawl  /of calf being weaned/   *blare, cry,
            blat, blate, bellow

 # e     low  /during feeding time/   *moo

 # e     whinny  /during feeding time/   *nicker,
            whicker, whinner, whinker, laugh

         feed) the cattle   *critters, creeters,
            stock

    m    feed) the fowls  /general term/   *fowl

 # e     a setting-hen   *hatching-hen, cluck, brooder,
            broody-hen
```

```
# e      chicken coop   /describe; for all the chickens?
         for mother hen and little chicks?  get
         coop for pronunciation/   *chicken house,
         hen house, hennery, jouguoir

                  ***

N        I must go and feed) the stock  /general term;
         normal terms; terms of affection and abuse/
         *beasts, beasties, critters

                  37

# e      wish bone   *lucky-bone, pulley bone, pull bone

# e      harslet  /comprehensive term for edible 'insides'
         of a pig or calf/   *haslet, chittlins,
         pluck, squin, liver and lights

N        giblets  /edible insides of a fowl/

MS T     intestines   *chittlins

#        feeding time   *fodder time, chore time

# e      calls to cows  /mark stress and intonation
         in all calls; note repetition!/
         to get them from the pasture   *come, boss!
         co-(w)ench!  sook(ie)!  soo(k)-cow!
         chay! co-ee!  co, boss!
         to make them stand still during milking
         *so! sah! histe! foot! saw, boss!
         saw (madam)!

# e      calls to calves   *sook, calf!  sook, sook!
         bossie!  calfie!

# e      calls to draft oxen  /to make them go left or
         right in plowing; to horses or mules?/
         *gee!  haw!

# e      calls to horses  /when getting them from the
         pasture/   *ku-jack!  co-jack!  kope!
         curp!  curph!  quop!  quopy!  quoby!  quowa!
         whistling

                  ***

N        craw  /of fowl/   *crop
```

38

```
#  e        get up!  /to start horses; to urge horses on/
                *gee up!  come up!  clucking

#  e        /to stop horses; to back them/   *whoa!
                back up!  hike up!

#  e        calls to pigs  /when feeding them/ *chook,
                chook!  poke!  pok!  suey!  suwee!  kong,
                kong, kong!  poo-wee!  soo-boy!  pi-goo(p)!
                pig(gie)!

#  e        calls to sheep  /when getting them from the
                pasture/   *coo-sheep!  coo-nan(nie)!
                kudack!  coday!  cade!

#  e        calls to chickens  /when feeding them/
                *chickie-chickie!  chick-chick!  kip-kip!
                koop-koop!

#  e        I want to) harness (the horses  /for driving?
                plowing?/   *tackle up, rig up, gear up

N           What is a 'team'?  /the horse or horse(s)
                and wagon?/

                        ***

       1    /calls to ducks/
T           /calls to turkeys/

N           hitch up  /to wagon or plow/   *hook up,
                ketch up

       m    /calls to animals to back up/

C           /calls to children at mealtime/

C           /calls from kitchen at mealtime/

C           /calls to summon friend from his house/

C           /calls to request the return of a ball on the
                street or playground/

C           /calls to attract attention/   *yo, hey, etc.

C           /calls or whistles to hail taxi/

C           /calls by newsboy/
```

39

```
   +        lines  /for driving; for plowing/   *reins

            reins  /for riding on horseback/

# e        stirrups

# e        the nigh horse  /horse on the left/   *near
            horse, lead horse, wheel horse, saddle
            horse, line horse, haw horse

N          go slow   *slowly

N          come quick!  /not 'come, quick!'/   *quickly

N          he's feeling bad   *badly

# e c      a little way (over   *ways, piece

                         ***

        m  /animal on the right/
L          traces  /for horse to singletree/   *tugs,
            trace chains

RTP  l o   cinch  /band that holds saddle on/

TP     o   feed bag  /bag attached to horse's head to
            feed him/   *nose bag, morral, muzzle

RTP        lariat  /rope with loop; rawhide or hemp?
            only for roping?/   *lasso, reata, roping
            rope, rawhide rope

N          reins  /from bridle to hames/
        m  /describe a yoke/
L          cart  /two-wheel?/

T      o   hackamore  /for leading horses?  for breaking
            wild horses?/   *rope halter

L          wheel
```

```
# e        a long way (to go    *ways, a fur piece

# e c      you can find that) anywhere(s)    *anyplace

N      o   he walked) backward(s)

       o   he fell) for(w)ard(s)

MSTP   c   ne'er a one  /any use of 'nary'?/    *nary
           a one, not a one

GT     c   I ain't done nothin'  /record other double
           negations/

N  #       we'll not see any more trouble,) e'er a bit
           *at all

MS     c   I didn't like it) noways    *at all, any

MS         he didn't give me) none, any

                        ***

P          it looks) good   *well

N          I didn't say) e'er a word

N          did he talk) any?

N          he talked) some  /=a little/

       o   anymore  /declarative and affirmative/
           *nowadays
```

```
           he'll have trouble,) like as not    *apt as not

# e        furrows  /trenches cut by plow/

# e        we raised a big) crop (of wheat

# e        we cleared (the land  /of shrubs, trees/
           *cleared up, shrubbed, swamped out

# e        second cutting  /of clover, grass/   *rowen,
           aftermath, lattermath

# e        a sheaf (of wheat   *a bind, bundle
```

```
MS  # e       shock (of wheat, corn   /how many sheaves?/
                *stook

    # e       forty) bushels (of wheat    *bushel

                        ***

U             stem rust   /on wheat; describe varieties/
                *black rust, red rust

L             new-ground   /a piece of land just cleared/
                *slashing
L             old-field   /any (abandoned) clearing?  Indian
                crop land?/   *old ground

SL            fog grass   /dry grass in spring/   *old fog

N             the grass is all) mowed   *mown

P             pick   /to harvest grapes/   *cut

P             pick   /to harvest walnuts/   *knock, pole,
                gather

       n      forty) quintals of fish   *quintal


                        42

    # e       oats is thrashed   *are

       o      you and I ('ll have to do it   *me and you

MS  m o       both of us   *all two of us

       o      he and I (are coming over   *him and me

N   t o       it's for) him and me   *he and I
       o      between) you and me   *you and I

N             you've got to do it.) I?  /emphatic/   *me

       o      it's I  /observe 'hit'/
              ... he
              ... she
              ... they

    m o       he isn't as tall) as I am   *as I be, as me

                        ***

S             /record usage on:  /em/ for 'him, her, it,
                them' and /i/ for 'he, she, it, they'./
       t      they asked) my wife and me   *I
```

```
     m      I'm not as tall) as he is    *as he be, as
                him

   m  o      he can do it better) than I can    *than me,
                than I

N            these are) the largest (apples we have
                *all the bigger

   #  e      two miles is) the farthest (he could go
                *all the farther, all the further

   #  e  c   it's yours,   *your
      c      ... ours   *ourn
      c      ... theirs   *theirn
      c      ... his   *hisn
      c      ... hers   *hern

MS #  e  c   when are) you (coming again  /pl.; is 'you-
                all' ever used as sing.?/   *youse, you'ns,
                'mongst-you, you-all

S  #  e      you-all's  /genitive/

MS #  e      who-all (was there?
MS #  e      who-all's (children were there?

MS #  e      what-all (did he say?
   #         what-all's  /possessive/

                         ***

N            he isn't any better) than you    *nor you

SL           John's  /attributive and absolute/
                *John's own
```

```
  o      they've got to look out) for themselves
              *theirselves, theyselves

m e o    he better do it) himself    *hisself
```

/Food items are highly variable and dependent on pecu-
liarities of local culture. Very often an item will be
remarkably productive in a small area and unproductive
outside it./

```
  # e      wheat bread  /in loaves/   *white bread,
              light bread, bread, pan bread

  # e      other kinds of bread made of flour  /prepa-
              ration, shape/   *rim, wasp nest bread,
              riz bread, yeast bread, biscuits, hot rolls,
              bannocks, poverty cakes, buns, potato bread,
              limpa, salt-rising bread

  #        a pan of) biscuit(s)

  #        corn bread  /in large cakes/   *johnny cake,
              corn pone, pone

    +      other kinds of bread and cakes made of corn
              meal  /preparation, shape; in frying pan?
              ashes?  on board in front of fire?  in fish
              grease? with cracklings from rendered lard?/
              *bread, spoon bread, awendaw, batter bread,
              egg bread, ash bread, ash cake, ash pone,
              hoe cake, flap-jack, corn dodger, johnny
              cake, corn duffy, grilled bread, cracklin'
              bread, fatty bread, hush-puppies, red-
              horse bread, corn sticks, muffins, corn
              cakes, tortillas, Indian bread
```

                            ***

```
SL         he) lighted him (a pipe   *himself
SL         can we) find us (a trail back   *ourselves

 L         do you want (a sandwich) on bread or bun?
              /is 'bread' used only of loaf bread?/

      n    hard tack  /hard bread on ship; stress?/
              *brewis
      n    dunch  /heavy bread without leaven/
  m n    the bread is dunchy   *soggy, klotsy
```

#		home-made bread and) bought(en) bread *baker's bread, town bread
N		sweet rolls /describe/ *buns, coffee rolls, sugar rolls
#		doughnut /preparation, shape; with baking powder? yeast? hole?/ *cruller, fried- cakes, fat-cakes, raised doughnuts, yeast doughnuts, olicook, riz doughnuts, croquignoles
#		griddle cakes /of wheat/ *pancakes, batter cakes, hot-cakes, flannel cakes, flapjacks, slapjacks, fritters, flitters, bang-bellies, damper devils
	# e c	two pounds (of flour *pound
	# e c	a cake) of yeast *east, emptins, cunnell
	# e c	yolk *yelk, yellow, red, glare
MS	# e c	the yolk is) yellow /name of the color/

***

	c	ryebread /varieties?/ *whole wheat bread
	c	/derogatory names for bread/
L		sinkers /biscuit? doughnuts?/
L		was(ps) nest /baker's bread? sponge cake?/
	m	bannocks /for human consumption? for animals? varieties?/
N		the bread is) molded *moldy, funked
T		brioche /small cake/ *tea cake
UP		spook yeast /liquid, home-made; grows in jar?/ *sourdough
	l	beignets /fried bread dough/ *langue de boeuf
	l	french toast *lost bread, pain perdu
	t	color
C		coffee cake /varieties/ *strip (with fruit prefixed); strudel (with fruit prefixed)

```
# e c    boiled eggs

# e      poached eggs  /how prepared?/   *dropped eggs

     +   salt pork   *side-meat, sow belly, sow bosom,
             salt butts meat, fatback, white meat, white
             bacon
     +   a side (of bacon  *flitch, slab, middling

MS   +   smoked pork  /smoked slated pork/   *bacon,
             smoked meat

     +   bacon rind  *skin, meat skin, hide

MS   +   bacon   *strip meat, breakfast bacon, fry,
             fry meat

N    +   jerked beef  *smoked beef, dried beef,
             jerky, salt-horse

   # e     sausage  /record familiar varieties/

   # e     butcher

   # e     the meat is)  spoiled

                    ***

     o   hard boiled eggs

P        recipe   *receipt

     c   what does 'soul food' mean?

     l   boiled shrimp  *boil
     l   stuffed crabs  *stuff

T    l   cracklings  /pork scraps, usually from
             rendered lard, cut up and fried/
             *gratins

C        /record cuts of beef ,pork, lamb, kinds of
             steak, kinds of packed fowl/
```

```
# e     head cheese  /are head cheese and souse the
                same thing?/   *souse, hogshead cheese,
                relishes
M       rollichies  /ground beef rolled in tripe,
                pickled, then sliced and fried/
M       vinkey  /corn meal and chopped liver cooked
                together, then sliced and fried/
MS   +  liver sausage   *liver pudding, liverwurst,
                liverel, white pudding
MS   +  blood sausage   *blood pudding, black pudding
MS   +  scrapple  /corn meal in juice from head cheese,
                liver sausage, etc./   *cripple, ponhoss

     +  the butter is) rancid   *frowy
# e     curdled milk  /thick sour milk/   *bon(n)ey-
                clabber, bon(n)ey-clapper, lobbered milk,
                loppered milk, clabber, thick-milk

# e     cottage cheese   *pot cheese, Dutch cheese,
                smear cheese, smear case, clabber cheese,
                sour-milk cheese, curd, home-made cheese,
                cruds

N       most cheese are (round   *most cheese is

        you better) strain the milk

     +  apple) cobbler  /baked in a deep dish; describe
                preparation/   *apple dowdy, pan dowdy,
                apple slump, deep-dish apple pie, deep apple
                pie, pot pie, bird's nest, family pie,
                apple grunt, apple Jonathan

                        ***

SL      minister's face  /hog's head with jowl meat
                removed/
LT   o  jowls  /hog?  human?/

     c  milk
NT   o  the milk is) blinky  /just turning sour;
                adjective?  noun?/   *tainted, sour,
                blue-john, turning
```

```
       l    condensed milk    *condense

P           frosting  /sweet coating of a cake/    *icing
       t    I must) ice (the cake    *frost
       t    caramel
T      o    chocolate bar
P           ice cream  /note stress/
N           gravy  /meat juice from steak or roast/
                *dish gravy, thin gravy


       l    boucherie  /gathering of two or more families
                to butcher a pig/
       n    puddings  /contents/
       l    /what is andouille?/
       n    rind  /bark on tree; atop faggot/
       n    /to strip covering off tree trunk/
       l    /list the meals of the day/

       l    fricasse  /stew made with chicken/
       l    gumbo  /brown soup of chicken, shrimp, etc.,
                thickened with file (gumbo file/
       l    okra gumbo  /the same with okra/    *okra fevi
       l    bouillon  /clear soup made with beef or chicken
                stock/
       l    bisque  /tomato gravy made with stuffed
                crawfish; other varieties?/
       l    courtbouillon  /highly seasoned tomato gravy
                made with fish (redfish)/
       l    sauce piquant  /highly seasoned tomato gravy
                made with meat or fowl/
```

                               48

```
MS     o    food    *vittles, rations

   # e      sauce  /sweet liquid served with pudding/
                *gravy, dressing, dip, dope

   # e      a bite  /food taken between regular meals;
                small or large quantity?/    *snack, piece,
                baiting, bait

   # e c    we ate (at six o'clock  /when did you eat?/
                *et, eat

   # e c    how often) have you eaten (today?    *et, eat, ate

   # e c    I'm going to) make some coffee  /how is the
                coffee prepared?/    *cook, boil, draw, steep

   # e c    a glass of water  /shape of glass?/    *tumbler,
                goblet
```

MS   o   the glass is) broken   *broke

                    ***

N   1   mess /enough beans or anything for one meal/
             white sauce /flour, water, and grease/
                *poor man's gravy, made gravy, cream sauce

L   applesauce /consistency; is it ever used as
                an epithet?/
L   a saucy child   *sass, sassy

S   tea /light evening meal/   *supper, lunch

NP   m   I'm going) to get supper   *make supper, fix
                supper
L   vanilla custard   *pop
       m   to make tea

C   /does sauce ever signify a dish of fruit served
                as desert?/
       t   percolator
       1   she empties the coffee) grounds   *grinds
C   coffee made with previously used grounds
       1   coffee au lait /coffee boiled with milk/
                *cafe au lait
C   /varieties of pie/
       m   dumpling /with meats; with fruit/

                    49

e c   I drank (a lot of it   *drunk, drinked

e c   how much) have you drunk?   *drank, drunken,
                drinked

N   m   soda pop   *soda, pop, tonic, soft-drink, dope

e c   sit down! /invitation to sit down at table;
                to relatives or intimate friends? to
                strangers?/   *draw up, set by

N   he was) sitting (at the table   *setting

e c   I sat down   *set, sot

e c   help yourself (to potatoes   *take out, take

MS   m o   I helped myself   *holp, holped

```
# e        I don't care for any  /when declining food;
           to intimate friends?  to host?/   *choose
```

***

```
L          please) pass the (potatoes   *(I'd) thank
           you for the potatoes

     m     corn meal
```

```
# e c      warmed-over  /of food cooked and served a
           second time/   *warmed-up, hot-over, hot

# e        chew   *chaw, champ, chomp

N          hard to digest

#          mush  /describe preparation!/   *hasty pudding,
           Indian pudding, turn mush, turn flour, kush,
           suppawn, spawn

N          fruit salad

# e c      vegetables  /home-grown/   *sass, garden sass,
           garden truck, garden stuff

# e        vegetable garden   *garden, kitchen garden,
           victory garden

     t     truck patch  /larger than garden/
     t     lawn  /grassed area around the house/   *yard
     t     mow the lawn   *cut the grass

MS   +     hominy  /coarsely ground corn/   *samp,
           grits, hominy grits
     +     lye hominy   *hominy, big hominy

S          rice
```

***

```
     l     left-overs  *restants

N          chauk  /chew audibly/   *champ, smack

LT         cush(-cush)  /of corn meal or corn bread crumbs?
           wheat bread?  fried grits?  does it contain
           onions, peppers, bacon scraps?  is it eaten
           with milk or gravy?/   *tack
```

```
        1     file   /powder made from dried leaves of
                     sassafras tree/

T       1     jambalaya  /rice cooked with black-eyed peas
                     and ham or hog jowl; other ingredients?  any
                     special occassions?/   *hoppin'-john, perlew,
                     pilau
        n     garden   /area behind dwelling, whether planted
                     in vegetables or not/   *backyard


                    51

        m     just) smell (that, will you   *smell of

              the molasses are (thick

 #            maple syrup   *(sugar) tree molasses

 #      c     genuine (syrup, leather, etc.

        o     sugar is sold) in bulk   *loose

 #            jelly

              salt and pepper

 # e          give me a(n) apple!

                    ***

N             molasses   *treacle
L             sop (syrup  /wipe plate with biscuit or bread/
                   *mop up, wipe up
L             zip (syrup), syrups,  /used only jocularly?/
                   *sop(s)
SL            long sweetening, short sweetening
                   /are these terms used for molasses and syrup?/

SL      1     bagasse  /pulp left from grinding sugar cane/
                   *pummie(s)

NSL           a(n) old man

        m     knife, knives
        m     fork
        m     don't fress!  /warning to children to mind
                   their manners at table/

        1     grinding season   /season when cane is cut/
                   *la roulaison
        1     /crane-like apparatus for loading cane/
```

1   *sugar mill   /place where juice is pressed
     out of sugar cane and manufactured into
     sugar/   *sugar house

1   cane knife   /tool, held in one hand, used for
     cutting cane, grass or weeds/

                    52

N   these here fellows   *these fellows, them
         fellows

e c   them there boys   *them boys, those boys

e c   it's) over there /in view? out of sight?/
         *back there, over yonder, back yonder

N   them's (the fellows I mean   *those are

N   that tree   *yon, yonder

e c   do it) this-a-way   *this way

e   what's that? /when failing to hear someone's
         utterance/   *how's that? how? he? he? hm?

                    ***

N   this here man   *this man

N   he went) that-a-way!   *that way

N   what kind (do you want? /more than two kinds
         involved/   *which

53

```
NP      m       whom (do you want?    *who

N               whom (did you talk to?    *who

N               he didn't tell me) whom (he voted for    *who

N               these are the sort of) girls (I like
                   *them's the kind of) girls what (I like

        e       a man) that's poor (has a hard life    *what's
                poor

   #            he's the man) who owns the orchard  /relative
                   pronoun in nominative case omitted/   *as
                   owns the orchard, owns the orchard

   # e          he's a boy) whose father (is very rich    *that
                   his father, his father, that the father
```

54

```
N               we grow) several kind(s) of apples
N               this kind of apple(s) is late   /referring
                   to one kind/   *these kind(s) of apples
                   are late

   # e          seed  /of a cherry/   *stone, pit

   # e          stone  /of a peach/   *seed, kernel, curl, pit

   #            cling-stone peach   *plum peach, press peach,
                   stick-stone, cleave-stone, hard peach

   #            free-stone peach   *clear-seed peach, soft
                   peach, clear-stone, free-seed

   # e          core  /of an apple/   *seed, chits
MS       +      snits  /dried pieces of apple/

MS       +      peanuts  /any distinction between those bought
                   shelled and those not?  between home prepared
                   and store-bought?/   *ground peas, goobers,
                   grubies, pinders, ground nuts, grounuts,
                   ground almonds

   # e          walnut shell  /hard inner cover/   *hull

   # e          the burr (of a nut  /outer cover/   *shuck,
                   shell, hull
```

***

```
P              apricot
U              Russian peanuts   *sunflower seeds
RP             peanut shell   *hull

L       o      shrivel

L              pignuts  /are they the same as hickory
                 nuts?/  *hickory nuts
R              piñon(s)  *Indian nut(s), pine nut(s)
LT    l o      pecan

T     l        praline  /flat sheet of pecan candy/   *pecan
                 patties, pipitorias

      m        burr  /outer covering of chestnut/
      m        shell  /inner covering of chestnut/
```

55

```
NP             almonds   *peach seeds, peach stone seeds

   #           the oranges

   #           they are) all gone   *all

   # e         radishes  *redishes

   # e c       tomatoes

MS   m o       potatoes  *Irish potatoes

MS   m o       sweet potatoes   *potatoes, yams, porto ricos,
                 jerseys

   # e c       onion   *ingern

   #           spring onions  *young-onions, green-onions,
                 shallot, scallion, rareripe, chibbole,
                 toppy onions, toppies
```

***

```
L              it ain't any more (in the box   *it ain't no
                 more, we're all out of it, we're fresh out

     l         green peas  /small green peas grown in spring
                 gardens/   *English peas

     o         okra
```

55A

```
        m       those cabbages are (big    *cabbage

  # e           to) shell beans    *hull

  # e           butter beans  /large, yellowish or green flat
                    seeds, not pods; distinct varieties?  are
                    yellow string beans called 'butter beans'?/
                    *lima beans, sivvy beans, sewee beans

MS        +       string beans   *sallit beans, green-beans,
                    snap beans, wax beans, beans

MS        +       greens  /of turnips, etc./   *sallit

          o       two) heads of lettuce   *head
   S              five head(s) of children
```

***

```
P                 to shell peas

C                 wax beans  /small yellow, in pod/   *butter
                    beans

RT    m o         Mexican brown beans  /other beans commonly
                    grown or used?/   *frijoles, pinto beans,
                    red beans

L                 we have) a passel of children
```

56

```
  #               husks  /on ear of corn/   *shucks, caps

  #               sweet corn  /served on cob/   *sugar corn,
                    mutton corn, green-corn, roasting-ears,
                    table corn

  #               tassel /top of corn stalk/   *tossel, spindle,
                    top-gallant

MS #              silk  /on the ear/   *tossel, corn beard, corn
                    mutton

      m           pumpkin

MS    +           squash   *simlin

  #               muskmelon   *mushmelon, cantaloupe

  # e             mushroom  /get stress/   *mushroon, mushyroom
```

***

```
       o    husk   /outer covering of a kernel of corn/

U           /does 'simlin head' occur as an epithet?/

C           cauliflower

       1    gourd
       1    maypop  /fruit of the passion flower/   *grenade
       1    merliton  /green or white pear-shaped vegetables
              which grow on vines/   *vegetable pear
       1    casbananne  /large cucumber shaped vegetable,
              usually preserved/   *cocumbre brazile
       1    cocumbre sent bon  /small sweet smelling
              wild cucumbers/

       o    black-eyed peas
```

57

```
  # e       toadstool   *frogstool, frog bench, frog table,
              fairy caps, black man's cap
  # e       he couldn't) swallow it   *swaller it

       o    cigars and cigarets

  # e       she was) singing and laughing  /enter other
              examples in -n or with the prefix a-/
              *a-singin', a-laughin'

N           I didn't) get to do it   *get around to doing it

MS   m o    I ain't) beholden (to nobody   *obligated

MS   m o    I can (do it  /stress on 'do'/

   # e c    I can't  /stressed/

   # e c    I done worked (all day  /only emphatic?/
              *I done and worked

S           he is) done dead   *already
```

***

```
T           gumbo  /thick soup usually containing okra;
              varieties?/

R           hard liquor  /distilled; legal or home-made?/
              *moonshine, firewater, hooch
```

N   apple jack   *apple brandy, cider, brandy

N   take a) swig /of whiskey/   *nipper, nip,
           slug, shot

                        58

MS   m   he belongs (to be careful   *ought to be

      m   you dassn't go   *you don't dast go, daren't go

MS   m   you had ought (to know   *ought

   # e o he hadn't ought to /negative of 'he ought to'/
           *oughtn't to, ortn't to

   # e   I) won't do it

MS   +   you) might have helped me   *maught've holp

S   + c I might could (do it /future? past?/
           *might, mout, may can, might can, may could

N   m I wish (you could come tonight   *wished

N   we'll go hunting,) come cooler weather
           *when come
                        ***

SL   we belong (to have a good garden   *ought to

N   I might a' could /in response to 'You
           couldn't help him'/

L   I mout and I moutn't   *I might and I might not

L   if he would have come, (it would have been
           *if he had come

N   I want in   *to get in

                        59

   #   screech-owl /small/   *squeech owl, squinch
           owl, skrinch owl, scrooch owl, scritch owl

MS #   hoot-owl /large; other kinds of owls?/
           *hoo-hoo owl

```
MS      +      woodpecker  /get kinds/   *peckerwood

N              we used to hunt) fox(es)

MS      +      skunk    *pole cat

MS # e         varmints  /define; any animals?  (small)
                  predators?  rats and mice?  lice and bedbugs,
                  etc.?/

   # e          gray squirrel   *quack, cat squirrel, (mountain)
                  boomer

        +      red squirrel  /get other kinds/   *fox squirrel

MS      +      chipmunk  /not pocket gopher/   *ground
                  squirrel, gopher, picket pin, grinnie

N       m      porgy  /a fish/   *porgee, paugie, pogie,
                  scup, scuppaug

                         ***

L              /is 'peckerwood' used as an epithet?
                  (for persons?)/

L              bird
N              nest(e)s

        l      coot  /ducklike bird often hunted in duck
                  season; does not have webbed feet/
                  *poule d'eau, poule doo

        l      gadwall  /common gray-colored Louisiana duck/
                  *gray duck, dos gris

        l      horned grebe  /ducklike bird that is able to
                  dive below the water and remain submerged
                  for long periods of time/   *diver, plongeur,
                  didapper
        l      gros-hec  /black-crowned night heron; has
                  thick, heavy bill/   *dos soir

N              there are no) bears (left in this section
                  *bear
        m      mouse; mice

        m      /is 'varmint' used of persons?/

L              black squirrel
```

```
SL          mole    *plow jogger

N           /what is a 'gopher'?/
    l m n   /list common local fish, especially edible
                ones; distinguish fresh and salt-water
                varieties/

        n   /trouting terms/

        m   /game animals/
        m   moose   /get plural/
        o   go fishing
        l   trawl   /to catch fish or shrimp in a large
                bag net pulled behind a boat/    *troll

      l o   trout lines   /stationary fishing lines, usually
                checked once a day/    *trot lines

        l   /fishing pole made of bamboo and string/
                *nigger pole


                        60

N           hard clam    *cohog, quahog, pequahog, round clam

MS #        oysters

    # e     bullfrog    *bull-paddocks, bull-paddies, bloody-
                noun, buddy-dunk

MS # e      peepers   /small green frog, piping noise/
                *March peepers, peewinks, treefrog,
                tree toad, grass frog, rain frog, grunois

    # e     toad    *toad frog, hop-toad, dry-land frog

    # e     earthworm   *angleworm, bait, mud worm,
                red-worm, fish worm, fishing worm, ground
                worm, rain worm, isses, day worm
        +   night crawler   /large earthworm/    *night
                walker, town worm, wiggler, john jumper,
                dew worm

MS      +   turtle   /in water?/   *turtle, cooter

MS      +   terrapin   /on land?/   *tarpin, cooter, gopher
                        ***

      l t   shrimp   /different kinds/
        l   /different types of oysters/
```

TP   o   horned toad /small flat lizard with horns on
head and back/   *horned frog

        o   <u>bait</u>
        o   /other kinds of bait/

UP   rattlesnake /get varieties/   *prairie
rattler, moss auger, massasauge, diamond
back, sidewinder

GURTPClo   crawfish   *crawdad, crab, crayfish
P   m   <u>salmon</u>

        l   bigainot /an edible deep-sea snail/
*perri-winkle

        l   lamprey /snake-like creature with four tiny
legs, usually found in ditches after a
heavy rain/   *lampeel

        l   fiddler crab /small crab with one pincer
smaller than another/   *fiddler

60A

  # e   <u>moth</u> /around candle/   *candle fly, miller,
moth miller

  #   <u>moths</u> /in clothes; get sing. and pl./

  # e   firefly   *lightning bug, fire bug, June bug

MS   +   dragon fly   *snake doctor, snake feeder,
darning needle, mosquito hawk, spindle,
sewing needle, ear sewer, sewing bug
  #   hornets /describe varieties; size, shape,
color, nest, sting/

  # e   <u>wasps</u> /size, shape, color, nest, sting/
*dirt daubers, masons, wans, wans-bees,
mud wasp

  #   yellow-jacket /wasp or hornet? nest in ground
only?/   *shacket, yellow-tails

***

TP o l   chigger /small insect burrowing in human
flesh/   *red-bug, jigger
      l   piss ants /big black ants that sting/   *piece
ants, pismire

```
N            bed-bugs    *bugs, chinch-bugs

L            mosquito    *skitter, skeeter

LR           praying mantis    *walking stick, darning
                needle, devil's horse
L            walking stick  /different from praying mantis?/
      l      devil's horse  /big black grasshopper with
                red wings; not mantis?/


                    61

N            locusts  /plural/

MS    l      grasshopper    *hoppergrass

   # e       minnows  /a bait/    *minnies, shiners,
                minnow fish, killie(fish), silvers

   # e c     spiderweb  /in house and outdoors/    *spider's
                web, cobweb, spider nest, dew web

   # e       roots

N            elm

      +      sugar maple    *sugar tree, hard-maple, rock
                maple

      +      maple grove    *sugar bush, sugar orchard,
                sap bush

NM #         sycamore   *button wood, button ball, plane
                tree

                    ***

L            katydid  /other names?/
      m      earwig

      n      caplin   *squid  /other baits?  plurals?/

L            harricane  /upturned tree with its roots and
                a water-filled root hole/
```

```
 #           cherry tree

 #           sumach

MS #          poison ivy    *poison oak, poison vine, mercury

 # e         strawberries

N        m   stem  /of strawberry/   *cap, hull

 # e         raspberries

N #          some berries are) poisonous   *poison

             mountain laurel   *laurel, ivy, spoonwood,
                spoonhunt

MS           rhododendron   *laurel

MS           magnolia   *laurel tree, cucumber tree,
                cowcumber

                          ***

   m n o     /common trees; juniper, larch, hackmatack,
                pine, poplar, popple, choke-cherry, oak/

N            linden   *basswood, lin-tree, lime tree

URT  l o     clump  /group of trees in open country; on
                prairie?  on hill?/   *grove, motte, bluff,
                cheniére

T        o   chapparal  /place where mesquite grows thick/
T        o   shinnery  /land where scrubby oak grows/

R            cottonwood   *alamo

R            aspen   *quaking asp, quaker, asp

R            service berries  /purple sweet edible berry
                with many seeds; large bush with narrow
                pointed leaves/   *sarvis berries; shad bush

     m n     /wild berries:  spice berries, blueberries,
                fox berries, cranberries, maidner berries,
                hurts, partridge berries/
N            daisy  /white petals/   *white weed
```

l   chinaberry tree   *china umbrella tree,
       umbrella tree, chinaball tree, chaney tree

n   kronik /small stunted tree/

n   rampike /large, weatherbeaten tree; sometimes
       killed by fire?/

n   starrigan /good standing tree, say, for
       cutting, short pieces of wood/

n   snotty var /evergreen tree that oozes gum;
       good for fires/ *vir

n   malldow /hanging white moss on var trees,
       as dead branches/

l n   piss-a-beds *dandelions, posies, bumblebee
       flowers, pis-en-lit

n   tuck /low bushes on barrens; 6 inches high?
       knee high?/ *gua-witty

l   cut grass *jaune coupon
l   paille fine
l   black-eyed susans *nigger tits
l   prêle /herb which looks like miniature bamboo;
       shoots are used to make tea/
l   water-lotus seeds *grains à violet
t   shrubs
o   bush

63

\# e c   I must ask) my husband *my man, the mister,
       my old man

\# e c   I must ask) my wife *my woman, the wife, the
       Mrs., my old lady

\# e c   widow *widow-(w)oman
\# e c   father
\# e   what do you call your father? /usual term
       and terms of affection/ *pa, paw, pop,
       popper, pappy, daddy, dad

\# e   what do you call your mother? /usual term and
       terms of affection/ *maw,ma, mommer

\# e c   parents

***

N   /Would you call John's wife 'Mary John'?/
  m widower

64

```
#  e        grandfather  /usual term and terms of affec-
                tion/   *grandpah, granpap, grampy, granther,
                gramps

#  e        grandmother  /usual term and terms of affection/
                *grammah, grammy, granny, gramps, gran

      m     our children (are still in school  /any special
                designation for small children?/   *young'uns,
                kids, chaps

N           pet names for child   *spouse, tad, tradge(t),
                hon, kid, tot, tyke, skeezicks, bubby,
                sissie, tunk

MS #        baby carriage   *baby buggy, baby cab, baby
                coach, buggy wagon

MS  m o     wheel (the baby   *roll, ride, air

MS  m o     he's) the grown-upest (of my boys
                /superl. of ppl./

   # e c    daughter

   # e c    girl

                         ***

      l     godfather
      l     godmother

SL          pet name   *basket name

SL          sister   *tittie

N           Would you call John's son 'little John', even
                if his name were George?

S           yard child  /define/   *yard son

      t     go cart   *stroller

C           son

C           boy
```

MC		she is) pregnant /term used by women, by men/ *big with child, expecting, in health, she (is) foot broke, she broke foot (her leg)
	#	midwife *granny, granny woman, godmother
	# e	the boy) resembles (his father /in looks? disposition?/ *takes after, favors, features, looks like, is the spitten image of, natured like
N	# e	she has) reared (three children *raised, brought up, fetched up, fotch up
N		she has to) look after (the baby *mind, tend, take care of, see after
M		you(re going to get a) whipping /to child/ *licking, smacking, skutching, skelping, trouncing, correcting, browsing, linting, larruping, tanning, blistering, thrashing, frailing, skinning, shellacking, switching, beating
	# e	Bob) grew (a lot in one year *growed
N	# e	you've) grown (big *growed
MS	# e	bastard /illegitimate child/ *woods colt, come-by-chance, catch-colt, old-field colt, volunteer, base-born (child), bush child, Sunday baby, buzzard egg

***

SL		pacifier *sugar tit, sugar rag, nipple
	1	traiteur /woman who treats warts, etc./ *traiteuse
C		/taboo items: normal, crude and jocular terms for sexual and excretory functions and organs, contraceptives,methods and devices, sanitary napkin, oral and anal air release, etc./

S   Mary is) a lovinger (child than Nelly
      /comp. of 'loving'/

\# e   <u>nephew</u>

\# e   <u>orphan(t)</u> /is word used only of children in
      an institution?/ *orphan child, orphan
      house child

\# e   <u>guardian</u> *guardeen

\# e.   her relatives *people, folks, kinfolks,
      folkses, home folks, kinnery

S   he is) no kin to her *no relation

MS m stranger /someone from out of community;
      someone never seen before/ *foreigner,
      new-comer, frenne

N   he is my) chum /of the same sex/ *buddy,
      pal, crony

         ***

TP   <u>partner</u> /used in address?/

SL   he is the) beatin'ist fellow

N m   there's a) <u>gentleman</u> (at the door

\# e   <u>Mary</u>

\# e   <u>Martha</u>

\# e   <u>Nelly</u>

N \# e <u>Billy</u>

\# e   <u>Matthew</u>

N   <u>Daniel</u> Webster

```
     # e c   Mrs. Cooper   /slow and fast form of Mrs. /
NP     m     Mrs. Brown

N      m     Miss Brown

N            Reverend Simpson    *(the) Reverend Mr. Simpson

       m     woman teacher    *school ma'am, school miss,
                teacher

S      +     jackleg preacher   /untrained, part-time/
                *yard ax

     # e c   your aunt
                        ***

       t     caller

L            Carl

L            Arthur

       o     Ralph

SL           Miss (Mary  /more familiar  form of address;
                to married women?  by whom used?/

R            jackleg (carpenter  /part-time?  unskilled?/

SL           circuit rider  /itinerant preacher/  *circus
                rider
```

68

```
            Aunt Sarah

N    m  o   Uncle William
            Uncle John

     #      General (Lee  /title, not primary stress/
N           general

            Colonel (Brown

N           Captain (Smith
            captain  /to whom used?/

   # e c     Judge (Marshall

   # e       student   *scholar, pupil

   # e       secretary
```

***

```
GURP   m    postman   *mailman

       o    rural route
P           the boy has a) paper route

C           alderman  /singular and plural/   *councilman

C           garbageman  /euphemisms  and ordinary terms/
```

69

```
N  #        the) selectman  /town officer; what town officers
                are there?/   *reeve, supervisor, trustee
            he's a) selectman

N           tourist   *tourister

            actress   *stage woman, show woman

   #        American

N     l     a(n) Italian  /record also nicknames/

N           nicknames for 'Irishman'

N           nicknames for 'Jew'

   #        Negro  /neutral terms/   *colored man, nigrah
```

```
    #          Negro   /derogatory and jocular terms/

S              master (John   /as used by Negroes to whites/

S              the poor whites   /white man's terms/
                 *Jackson whites, common people, trash,
                 red-necks

S              the poor whites   /Negro's terms/   *poor
                 buckra, crackers

    #          a rustic   /derogatory terms and neutral terms/
                 *mountain boomer, yahoo, cracker, hill
                 billy, swamp angel, mossback, countryman,
                 backwoodsman, coveite, hayseed, ridge runner,
                 jackpine savage, hay shaker, hayman,
                 outharbor-man, john wills, farmer

                           ***

SL             justice of the peace   *j.p., squire
SL        m    /county or parish officials/   *warden

SL             squire (John   /only of large landowners?
                 by whom used?/

          m    summer people   /neutral and derogatory terms;
                 used only of Americans?/

Q              town clerk

S              medicine show   *minstrel show

N              traveling salesman   *drummer, runner, hustler

RP             cowboy  /only riders?  any ranch hand?/
                 *bronco buster, waddy, cowpoke, cowhand

RT             hand  /on a farm or ranch/   *cowboy, cowhand,
                 cowpoke, puncher, waddy, buckaroo, rider,
                 wrangler, hand, hired man

RP             migratory worker  /neutral and derogatory
                 terms/   *drifter, boomer, floater

T              Mexican  /neutral and derogatory terms; different
                 categories?/   *greaser, Meskin, pepper belly,
                 pilau, wetback
T              Tex-Mex  /Texan of Mexican ancestry/
                 *Spaniard, Spanish-American
```

```
N              /nicknames for 'French-Canadians'/    *pea
               soupers, frogs, Frenchies, canucks

LT        1    Acadian French    /neutral and derogatory terms:
                  do you distinguish between Creole and Cajun?/
                  *cajun, coon, creole, bougalie
LT             What is a Creole?
          1    negriller    /white man who associates with Negroes/
N              mulatto    *yellow man, high brown, high yellow

SL             (Negro) mammy    *nurse, da

SL             Gullah  /a dialect?  people?/    *Geechee, Geech
          1    /a North Louisianan/
L              red-bone    /Negro-white or Negro-Indian mixture?/
                  *croatan, creole, melungeon, Jackson white,
                  brass ankle
          o    an Indian  /also nicknames/

C         o    /terms for people recently of other nationali-
                  ties/


L              farmer

RP             out in the sticks    *out in the toolies, out
                  in Kansas, out in the badlands, out in the
                  jimsengs
          o    /a person from the back country/
          n    tally-man  /person with dark skin/    *jackatar,
                  jacks

          l    /farmer who works on shares/

          o    hired (man

          o    /first legal white settlers in Oklahoma after the
                  run/

          o    sooners  /persons who jumped the gun/
```

70

```
Q           it's) almost (midnight    *nigh, well-nigh,
              nigh onto, near, nearly, pretty near

MS          I) almost fell down    *like to've fallen
              down, like to fell

N       m   you were not) far off    /nearly right/

    #       just a minute

    # e     how far (is it to ...?

    # e     look here!  /exclamation; seriously or
              jestingly?/   *look-a-here, look it here
```

71

```
    # e     how often (do you go to town?

NP   e m    either you or I (will have to do it    *me or
              you one, you or either me

N       m   neither you nor I (can do anything about it

    #       I'm not going to do it!)  Nor I either.
              *neither, me neither

    # e c   forehead

    # e c   the) right ear

    # e c   beard

    # e c   mouth

MS # e     tooth, teeth

    # e     gums
```

***

```
L           I; my; your

SL          skin  /human/   *hide
```

72

```
  # e c    palm (of the hand   *pan

MS # e c    fists

  # e c    joint

  # e c    chest   *breast

  # e      shoulders

MS     m    the shins   *shanks

MS     +    the haunches  /define/   *hunkers, hunkles

N           stout   *pursy, pussy

       m    peaked  /as the result of ill health/
            *skinny, scrawny, thaveless, poor, sickly,
            pimpin', pindlin', puny, crawny-bone,
            strawny-bone
```

***

```
       n    slink  /very thin person/   *rames, skeleton

       n    armpits  /hallows under arm/   *oxters
```

73

```
            /get definitions for all/

       e    strong   *stout, husky, robust

     m o    good-natured   *clever, kind, admirable,
            pleasant, likely, common

     m o    he's so) awkward  /referring to physical
            appearance/   *ganglin', gawny, gorming,
            clumsy, gawky

N           that) awkward fellow!   *gawking gander, old
            cow, lobster, fumble-head, lunkhead, footy-
            head, stumble bum, Joe gum

N           he is quite) skillful at (plowing, carpentering,
            odd jobs   *a hand at, clever, handy, knacky,
            sleighty, a soon man
```

```
    m n     that fool!  /only of men?  of women?/
            *dough head, dunderhead, fool head,
            leather head, leather ears, lummox, cow,
            dub, dumbbell, goof, a born(ed) idiot,
            cracky person, gumel, stun pull

NU    l     he is a) tight-wad  /one who holds on to what
            he has?  one who gets the most out of
            others?/  *skinflint, crapper, greedy-gut,
            a cubbidge person

N     l     he's so) dull   *slow, logy, craque bine,
            bête

                        ***

TP    o     he has the) strength (of an ox

SL          common  /is 'common' ever used in a compli-
            mentary sense?/  *friendly, affable

P     l     lazy   *no-count, shiftless

      m     supple   *lively, active

UPL   o     he's so) stingy   *tight, chinchy, chintzy

      t     tump  /knock something over/   *tip, dump

P           lazy   *unambitious, no-account, onery, ornery

C           /a procurer of women/
C           /a house of prostitution/

C           /a sexually indiscreet female/
C           /a sexually overactive female/
C           /a sexually overactive male/

C           /a female homosexual/
C           /a male homosexual/
C           /a loafer/

C           /an alcoholic/
```

```
# e        she's) quite lively  /of young people?
           old people? both? get both adj. and
           qualifier/   *right peart, spry, brash,
           peppy, trappy, chipper, ficety (of
           children)

MS    o    uneasy

# e c      I'm) afraid  /temporary or habitual/  *scared,
           scary, afeared, scairt, all of a shiver

MS    m    she) used to be (afraid

# e c      she) didn't use to   *usen't to

N          she's too) slovenly (for me  *dutchy,
           tacky, sloppy, mussy, slouchy, dowdy, slack
           and nasty, gommy, messy

# e c      careless

# e        queer  /what does it mean?/

N #        don't be so) obstinate  *stubborn, set, sot,
           pig-headed, ornery, contrary, cracky,
           jumptious, bull-headed, mule-headed,
           hard-headed

                        ***

NC         chippie  /immoral woman/   *mean woman, old
           bat, old bag, fancy woman, sporting woman


      t    mess  /minor accident; as in spilling something/

L          it's) gaumy   *sticky
```

75

```
#          touchy  /easily offended/  *ficety, testy,
           touchous, fretful, short-patient

# e        he got awfully) angry   *mad, het-up, ashy,
           ugly, owly, shirty, mean, (se)vigrous

N          he was as mad as) a wet hen  /crazy?  angry?/
           *a bull, a hatter, a hornet, all get-out
```

N   he was) all excited /with expectation/
                  *all of a biver, all (of) a tremble, all
                  aflutter

N   m   the sea is) <u>calm</u> (today

MS # e   <u>keep</u> <u>calm</u>! /when used?/

   # e c   tired, exhausted /normal and strong terms/
                 *fagged out, perished, beat out, tuckered
                 (out), used up, done up, done in, petered
                 out, kilt, give out, whipped, pooped, all
                 in, bushed, blowed

   # e   he is) worn out   *wore (slam) out, tore in
                 two, broke in two

N   he is) chronically ill   *bad off, ailing,
                 afflicted, enjoying poor health

                      ***

      1   a face /look of displeasure/ *babine,
                 grimace, frimousse
UR   the stream got) riled up   *roily, roiled
                 up

S   he's) <u>a-rarin'</u> (to get you

UP   1   duck bumps *goose bumps, goose pimples,
                 goose flesh

S   we had a) <u>torn-down</u> good time

      o   <u>quiet</u> <u>down</u>

```
# e c   she) got sick   *took sick, was taken sick,
              was took sick

N      m    he is) some better   *somewhat, a little,
              a mite, doing all right

N          he is still) in bed   *a-bed

       m    he will be well again) by and by   *bumbye,
              bimebye

# e c   he) caught a cold   *caught cold, took cold,
              taken, take, ketched cold

# e c   I'm) hoarse

# e     he has a) cough

S          drowsy   *sleepy

S          wake up  /intransitive/   *rouse

S          wake up  /transitive/   *rouse

                    ***

L          he fainted   *fell out

L          he might) faint   *fall out

N          he was) cured
       l    croup  /a severe case of hoarseness/
       l    what's wrong) with you   *for you
       m    when she gets sick she) complains   *grunts

       m    go to sleep   *get asleep
```

```
# e c   haven't you) taken (your medicine yet?   *took,
              tuck

   + c    I) took (it this morning   *taken, takened,
              tuck

# e c   deaf   *deaf of hearing, deef, dif, hard of
              hearing

N      l    fever  /differentiate ordinary fever and
              malaria/   *the chills, the shakes, chills
              and fever, a turn of chills
```

```
N              what is the 'ague'?    *aguer

  # e c    he sweat (hard    *sweated

  # e c    boil /discharging/    *cattair, raisin',
                risin'

  # e c    pus   *matter, corruption, humor

      m    my hand) swelled up   *swole

      m    it is) swollen   *swelled up

                      ***

SL         buck fever   *buck ague(r)

SL         water /in a blister/   *humor

      l    bobo /child's name for a sore/   *hicky
      m    gout


                      78

  # e      wound /noun/
N          an inflamed wound   *angry wound, sore, bobo

  # e      proud flesh /stress/

      m    iodine

     m o   quinine

     m o   he) died /neutral and veiled terms/   *passed
                away, left us, passed on, departed this life

           died /crude terms/   *passed out, pegged out,
                kicked the bucket

  # e      I don't know what) he died of   *with, from
                /formal and jocular terms/

  # e      cemetery   *graveyard, burying ground,
                churchyard, burying yard, burying plot,
                potter(s) field

                      ***

N          diarrhea   *pantod, a running off, colic, the
                (back-door) trots, the runs, the G.I.'s

C          funeral parlor   *mortuary, undertaker's

SL         I) buried me (a son   *myself
```

79-80

79

```
    # e      casket    *coffin, pinto

MS  m o      funeral    *a burying

    # e c    they are in) mourning    *taking on

             pretty well  /in response to 'how are you?!/
                *pretty good, common, tolerable,
                middling

    # e c    don't worry!

    #        rheumatism    *rheumatiz, rheumatics, arthritis
N   # e c    rheumatism is (painful    *rheumatiz are,
                rheumatics are

N            the) mumps is (dangerous  /is it' or 'they'
                used of 'mumps'?/   *(the) mumps are

    #        diphtheria

    #        jaundice    *yellow jaundice, janders, yellow
                janders
```

                           ***

```
L            measles is (annoying    *are
```

80

```
    #        appendicitis    *cramp colic, locked bowels,
                inflamation of the bowels

N      m     he has) tuberculosis    *t.b., consumption,
                the con, the connie, the failing-disease,
                consumptious

    # e      vomit  /neutral terms/   *purge, puke,
                skin a goat, vomick, heave(up), cack,
                sick, spew, cascade, up-swallow, be ill

    # e      vomit  /crude and jocular terms/

    # e      he is sick) at his stomach    *to, in, on, of

    # e      he came over) to tell (me about it   *for, for to

N            you) ought for take (it easy   *to take
```

                    ***

SL   I'd like) to keep it   *for keep

N   I've got orders) not for to leave (you
               *not for leave, not to leave

N   I belong (to have it   /=I deserve to have it/

                    81

N # e   I shall be (disappointed if he doesn't come
               *I will

N # e   we shall be (glad to see you   *will be (proud)

N   +   I'll) go and spank (you   *take and spank,
            up and spank, spank

N   how is it that (you're here?   *how come

   #   he is) courting her   *going with, walking
            out with, sitting up to, a-talking to,
            keeping company with, sparking, spark it
            with, paying 'em address, rushing, (heavy)
            dating, sweet on, going steady

      m o   her boy friend /normal and jocular terms/

      m o   his girl friend /normal and jocular terms/
               *steady, thrill, doney, docksey, jewlarky

        m   kissing   *bussing, smootching, necking,
            spooning
                    ***

N   I better see what is still) to be done
               *to do

L   don't you go and do that   *take and do, up
            and do, do

N   o   his fiancee *best girl, wife, wife-to-be,
intended future madam, future Mrs.

\# e   she turned him down /serious and jocular
terms/ *she gave him the sack, the gate,
the ax, the mitten; threw him over, jilted
him, kicked him, turned him off, throwed
him down, broke off (with him)

\# e   married *hitched, spliced, jumped the
broomstick

   +   best man *waiter, groomsman

   +   bridesmaid *waiter

\# e   shivaree /noisy, burlesque serenade after a
wedding; describe; must one of the couple
have been married before? is it ever used
to signify community displeasure?/
*serenade, belling, dish-panning, skimmelton,
callathump, reception, horning, bull-banding,
drumming, salute

   m   I was) up in (Boston, Hartford, etc. /use verb
of rest, not of motion/ *up to, down in,
down to, over in, over to

   m   he lives) up at (the Browns *up to, over
at, over to

N   o   a big social affair *goings-on, doings, frolic,
lark, junketing, dingfad, a social, a big
to-do, blow-out, cat fight, kitchen junket,
kitchen tunk, shindig, kit and caboodle

\# e   the whole crowd /depreciative terms/ *bilin',
kittle and bilin', kit and bilin', gang,
mob, outlay, layout, bunch

                  ***

   1   common law marriage /to live together without
benefit of clergy/ *jump the broomstick,
macorner

N   they) were divorced *got a bill

   m   wedding gift *house stire

L   1   I'll) stand for (you /at a wedding, as best
man or bridesmaid/ *stand up with you,
serve

l   to visit /go to see neighbors, friends or
relatives/ *veiller

l   always on the go /expression used to describe
a person who is constantly visiting/ *has
a foot in the roads, rodailler

l   to pass by one's house /to call for someone/
make a pass

83

\# e   a <u>dance</u> *ball, hoe-down, a German, a
breakdown, frolick, shindig, hop, house
dance, kitchen dance, fais-de-do

N   two) couples *couple

m o   school) lets out (at four o'clock *turns out,
is over, gets out, leaves out, closes

m o   when does school) start? /after vacation/
*begin, commence, take up, take in

he) skipped class *played hookey, bolted,
hooked Jack, laid out, bagged school

\# e   <u>education</u> *learning, book learning

N   <u>class</u> *room

\# e   <u>college</u>

M \# e   first grade *first class, primary, first
reader

* * *

T   I'll draw another) <u>card</u>

T   I have) an appointment (at two *date,
engagement

n   <u>moocher</u> /one who plays hookey/

n   be promoted /go from one grade to a higher
one/

t   <u>university</u>

t   crayon *crayola, coloring crayon

84

```
# e        library

# e        post office

# e c      hotel

# e        theater    *opera house, show

N          we were in a) moving picture house
              *movie house, movie, theater

# e c      hospital

# e c      nurse

NM         railroad station   /contrast with bus station;
              try for four-stress items/   *depot, railway
              station
```

                              ***

```
      t    motel    *motor court, autel

C          political influence    *clout, pull, drag

C          /city employees who don't work/

C          air port    *air field
C          Midway
C          O'Hare Field

C          neighborhood store  /describe/   *delicatessen,
              grocery store
C          large grocery store   *supermart, market

C          office building, bloc
C          The Merchandise Mart    *The Mart

C          police station    *precinct
C          night stick    *billy

C          squad car    *prowl car
C          wagon    *paddy wagon, maria

C          fire house   *fire station, stationhouse,
              fire hall
C          fire truck  /describe/   *fire engine, hook-
              and-ladder
```

85

```
N       +       public square   *common, green, park, place,
                plaza, town square  /get names of parti-
                cular greens, parks, etc./

N               I live three) blocks (from here   *streets,
                squares, a five minutes' walk

T      m o      kitty-cornered  /of walking across intersection
                or lot/  *catter-cornered, catty-wampus,
                zig-zag, caper-cornered, bias-ways, antigodlin,
                antigoglin, antisigoglin

U      m o      /of furniture standing at an angle to the wall/

N    #          on the) street car   *trolley car, trolley,
                surface car, tram car, tram, electric car

     #          I) want to get off (at the next corner
                *want off

       +        county seat   *county capital, shire town,
                county site, county town, parish seat

     m o        the Federal) government

     #          Civil War   *the Rebellion, War between the
                States, War of the States, Confederate
                War, Yankee War, War of Secession

   # e          law and order   *law-r and order

     m o        the murderer was) hanged   *hung

N      m        he) hanged (himself   *hung

                          ***

C               elevated railroad   *L

UT              sashaying  /diagonally? zigzag? strutting?/
                *antigodlin, antigoglin, slabbing, going
                cattywampus, cattywampus, catty-cornered,
                catty-wompsun

N               he lives) on (Main street   *in

P               peninsula

       t        police
       t        policeman  /normal and derogatory terms/
```

86

/Chiefly for pronunciations/

		New England	*the Eastern States
		Massachusetts	
N		Connecticut	
N		Rhode Island	
N		Maine	
N		New Hampshire	
N		Vermont	
	#	New York /state/	*York State
M		New Jersey	
M	#	Pennsylvania	
M	#	Ohio	
MS		Maryland	
MS	#	Virginia	
	#	North Carolina	
MS	#	South Carolina	
	#	Georgia	
	#	Florida	
MS	#	c	Alabama
MS		c	Louisiana
MS	#		Kentucky
	t o c		Tennessee
	#	Missouri	
MS	#	Arkansas	
N	#	Texas	
N	RP	California	

***

RP		Arizona
RP	o	Colorado
U		Dakota
RP		Idaho
GUTP	o	Illinois
GTC	o	Indiana
UP	o	Iowa
	o	Kansas
GUT	o	Michigan
U		Minnesota
	c	Mississippi

R			Montana
U			Nebraska
RP			Nevada
R			New Mexico
RP			Oregon
RP			Utah
RP		o	Washington *Washington State
U	t	o	Wisconsin
R			Wyoming

/sentimental terms for one's home state/

n	Labrador /stress: also in phrases as to the Labrador/
n	Newfoundland /stress/
n	Newfoundlander
m	Nova Scotia

m	Annapolis County
m	Lunenberg County
m	Queens County
m	Shelburne County

87

N	m		Boston
N			New Haven
N			Springfield
MS	#		Baltimore
MS	#		Washington
M	#		Philadelphia
MS			Charleston
S			Asheville
MS		+	Louisville
	#	+	Cincinnati
	#	+	Chicago
MSP		o	St. Louis
MS	#	+	New Orleans
			Ireland
P			France
			Russia
NP			Asia

***

R		Albuquerque
L		Alexandria
SL		Atlanta
T		Austin
L		Baton Rouge
	c	Birmingham
C		Cairo /Illinois/
R		Cheyenne
T		Dallas
R		Denver
U		Des Moines
C		Des Plaines /Illinois/
GU m c	o	Detroit
U		Duluth
	o	Enid
P		Eugene /Oregon/
	o	Guthrie
	m	Halifax
R		Helena
L		Homer
L		Houma
T		Houston
	t	Indianapolis
	o	Kansas City
R		Laramie
P		Los Angeles *L.A.
	o	McAlester
	o	Miami
U		Minneapolis
P		Mohave
L		Monroe
	o	Muskogee
	o	Oklahoma City
U		Omaha
	o	Ponca City
R		Pueblo
T		San Antonio
P		San Bernardino *San Berdoo
P		San Francisco *Frisco
P		San Jose
R		Santa Fe
RP		Seattle
	o	Shawnee
L		Shreveport
	n	St. John's
P		Tulare
	o	Tulsa
P		Vallejo
	o	Wichita
P		Yosemite

```
        m      /neighboring towns and villages/

        c      /record names for natives of various states
                  and cities/

        t      Gulf (of Mexico)
GUTC    o      Canada
     e  m      England
S              Panama

C              Northside
C              Near Northside
C              Southside
C              Southwest Side
C              Westside
C              The Loop
C              Downtown    *Uptown
C              Back-of-the-yards
C              Bughouse Square   /the small park facing the
                  Newberry Library/

P              Geary (Street  /in San Francisco; in other
                  areas substitute appropriate local names/
P              Kearny (Street
P              Greenwich (Street
```

```
        m o    ten) miles    *miles

N       m o    a hundred) rods (from here   *rod

        m      I don't know as I want to   *if, whether

N              I don't care) just so (you get back soon
               *so long as, as long as

N   # e        it seems) like (he'll never pull through
               *as if, as though

    # e        I won't go) without (he goes   *'douten,
               (un)less, 'lessen

    c m o      instead of (helping me

N       m      whilst I (was talking to him   *while

N              I don't know) but what (I better   *but,
               but that

N              I wouldn't go to his house to stay) and him
               not there   *if, iffen, with

N              he went out,) and his overcoat on his arm
               *with

    # e        I like him) 'count of (he's so funny
               *because, becuz, cuz

N              it's tired I am  /=I'm very tired/

                    ***

N              he went away  /to some other part of the U.S./
               *abroad, to furrin parts

N       o      a hundred) yards (from here   *yard

L              a country mile  /jocular expression for a
               considerable distance/

L              it's) three acres from here  /'acre' as a linear
               measure/

SL             the Lord help me) do she smell it   *if, iffen,
               effen
```

```
SL              if you go (I won't stay    *an you go, if,
                   iffen

L               being as you asked me    *being, since,
                   being (as) how
```

89

```
N               I'm after writing a letter   /=have just
                   written/

MS       +      Baptist

   # e c        they joined (the church

   # e          God  /as pronounced in church/   *master

   # e          my) God  /an oath/

N               Mass

   # e          sermon

N        o      psalm

MS # e          music

MS # e          beautiful

         m      ballad  /ever for 'hymn'?/   *song ballit

                church will be over) agin I get there
                   *by the time
```

                          ***

```
L        o      Methodist; Catholic; E)piscopalian; Presbyterian
                   *other names for churches
L               parochial school   *paroshial

N               he was converted  /in a revival meeting/
                   *got religion, came through, went forward

         o      sing
L               hymnal    *hymn book, song book

         n      turn coat  /person who changes from one
                   church to another/

         n      to turn coat

C        n      micks, bluds  /what religious groups in town
                   or area?  have others ever come?  nicknames?/
```

     t   stereo   *hi-fi, record player, phonograph

                        90

e   devil /also veiled and jocular terms/
                 *the bad man, the booger man, the black
                 man, old Harry

e   spooks   *ghosts, spirits, haunts, fraids,
                 poky spots, boogers, Plateye, rawhead-
                 and-bloody-bones, the clavers

e c   a haunted house

e   it's) rather (old   *kind of, sort of, middling

e c   I'd rather (not go

N   it's awfully (cold   *terribly, right,
                 monstrous, fearfully, powerfully, powerful,
                 right smart

      m o   I'm mighty glad to see you! /record intonation/
                 *awfully, very, right proud

                       ***

N   I'm) good and hungry   *powerful hungry,
                 awfully, mighty

L   if I had my druthers (I wouldn't go   *ruthers

L   1   it's) cold cold /=very cold; notice if
                 adjectives are repeated for intensity/
L   it's) very cold

```
#              certainly!  /strong affirmation; get all
               affirmative responses used in conversation;
               record intonation and stress, both normal
               and emphatic/  *sure!  you bet!  of
               course!  yes, indeed!  surely!  I mean!

N              why, yes!

       m       I sure can   *certainly

#              habitual forms of 'yes'

#              yes, sir; yes, mam  /do you habitually say
               'yes, sir' and 'yes, mam' or simply 'yes'?/

       m       well!  /hesitation/

N      m       a lot of fun   *(dead-) loads, stacks, heaps,
               scads, slews, no end, bokoos, piles

N      m       a little (bit

S              he) purely (dreaded the place   *pinely,
               pointedly, plumb

N      m       that's) enough!

N      o       is it) really so?
               real cold, real good

               them's) real (dogs   *rale, some dogs

                         ***

SL     l       he owns a) right smart (of land   *a good
               deal, right much, plenty

SL     o       it's a little (different, high, etc.
               *a mite

P              no  /habitual forms of negation; note intona-
               tion/
```

m o   damn (it)! /arrange in order of emphasis;
              what expressions are peculiar to women?/
              *blame it! dang it! consarn ye!
              custom! dad-burn! -dern! -gum! darn
              it! dern it! dog-gon! dog take it!

m o   for the) lamb's sake! /ever used by men?/
              *land sakes! sakes! sakes alive! my
              goodness! for goodness' sake!

c o   shucks! /exclamation of impatience or disgust/
              *tarnal! botheration! tarnation!

m o   the idea!

N   why! /exclamation; stressed/

N   don't curse (like that!

\#   how are you? /to an intimate friend;
              intonation!/

\#   how do you do? /to a stranger; intonation!/
              *how be you?

***

c   /exclamations and epithets of contempt; the
              worst you've used; the worst you've heard/

N   good-bye! /only when parting for a long time?/

\# e   come again! /to a visitor/   *(you-all)
              come back, (hear)!

N   hurrah!   *hurray!, hurraw!

e +   Merry Christmas! /among adults? among
              children? by Negroes?/ *Christmas gift!
\#   Happy New Year! *New Year's gift!

***

N   don't mention it!   *you're welcome

NSL   I'm much) obliged *obleeged

n   Christmas box /something given at Christmas/

	m o	I think (I'll have time *guess, suppose, reckon, allow, calculate, figure
NC	m	grocery store /neighborhood? large? distinguish/ *grocery, delicatessen, supermarket
	m	I had to do some) shopping (downtown *trading
	o	he <u>wrapped</u> it up (in paper *wrop
MS	m o	I) <u>unwrapped</u> (it *onwrapped
N		how much do you charge for it? /in a store; intonation/ *take, ask, tax; how much are you getting? how much is that? how much does it come to?
N		how much do you want? /in a private deal/ *what are you holding it at? what's it worth to you?
	m	sell) at a <u>loss</u> *below cost
MS #	e c	it) <u>costs</u> (too much *costes
#	e	the bill is) <u>due</u>
#	e	pay) the <u>dues</u>

**

SL		I don't think (so /is 'so' omitted?/ *I don't guess (so); I don't believe (so)
R		how much did you) waste (for that dress? /is 'waste' used in normal contexts without implying carelessness or extravagance?/ *spend
TP	l o	racket store /store where all kinds of cheap goods are sold; town or country?/ *general store, dime store, Noah's Ark, Woolworth's
R		money /silver only? get popular names of silver coins/ *hard money, silver dollar, iron man, dinero, buck; two, four, six, eight bits
N		auction sale *vendue
L		that will be (twenty-five cents

```
N            have) in stock    *on hand

T       l    lagniappe  /bonus or gift when a purchase is
             made or a bill is paid/   *pilon, brautus

        n    tilly  /small amount (as of molasses) ever
             and above quantity purchased   *tally

        n    bait  /free gift presented to the first
             buyer/   *hansel


                    95

  # e c    borrow

N            it isn't of much) value

MS #         money is) scarce (nowadays    *hard come by,
             tight

    m        the boys) coast (down the hill
             *sled-ride, bob, slide

  #          coast lying down   *coast belly-bunt,
             belly-bust, belly-bumps, belly-gut,
             belly-flop

  # e        somersault   *somerset

  # e c      I swam across   *swum

  # e c      he dived in   *dove, div

                    ***

SL           I could) scarcely (see him

N            he won (five dollars  /on a bet/   *win,
             winned

UP           marbles   *migs, mibs, miggles, mibbies,
             agates, peewees, threaders, moons

UP           starting line  /in marbles/   *taw, taw line,
             lag line, lagging line, shooting line

    n o      belly-flasher  /a dive flat on stomach/
             *belly buster

        n    Milkmaid's Path  /band of stars across sky/
             *milky way
        n    copying  /children jumping from one piece
             of floating ice to another/   *cockying,
             running the pans
```

```
n     hide and seek    *hidy
n     /can informant recite "Ducks and Drakes"?/
n     /other games heaving rocks/
n     mummers   /children or grown-ups who dress
          up at Christmas and visit homes/   *janses,
          fouls
n     /what do children do on St. Stephen's Day?
          (Dec. 26, or Boxing Day)/
```

96

```
# e       he was drowned    *drownded

    +     the baby) creeps (on the floor    *crawls
N   o     he) crept (close    *crope, crup

# e c     he) climbed (up a tree
              *clum, clome, clim, clam, clom, cloom

N # e     I have often) climbed up    *clum, clome, clim

    +     crouch    *scrooch down, scrutch, hunker down,
              squat

# e c     she) kneeled (down    *knelt

# e       I'm going to) lie down   *lay down

                    ***

N         don't step (on the vines    *tromp
```

# e	he) lay in bed (all day	*laid a-bed
# e	I) dreamed (all night	*dremt, dremp
# e c	I woke up (early	*wakened, waked up, roused, got awake
N	you better) pitch in	*link in, turn to, hop to, hump to it, hump yourself, lend a hand, give a hand
N	he ran like) a house a-fire	*sixty, a scared rabbit, all get out
# e c	stamp (the floor	*stomp
# e	may I) take you home? /on foot or in a vehicle?/	*see you home, carry you home, bring you home
# e c	pull	
# e c	push	

***

U	hurry up!	*hurry on
N	he) lay down (in the grass	*laid down
L	stamp (it /with a rubber stamp/	
L	escort /to a social event/	*take, carry, drag, accompany
L	I carried her (to the dance	*took
L	I'll) bring (you home in my car /said of or at the place, not at home/	*take

```
# e        I lugged (a bag of meal, etc.
               *packed, toted, hiked, sacked

# e c      don't you touch it!

N          I'll have to) repair (the table, harness,
               etc.   *fix, mend, coggle, cobble, 'tend to

# e        go bring (me a knife   *fetch, get, find

N          the children play tag   *play catchers

# e        goal  /in children's games; in hocky; in
               basketball or football/   *gool, base,
               home, den

# e        catch (the ball   *ketch

# e c      who) caught (it?   *ketched, kotch, kitched

N      m   I have never) caught (it yet   *ketched

                       ***

L          stand (you) up  /break a date/   *dayen you
               out

L          go bring the chicken some feed   *take
L          bring this by (the postoffice on your way
               home   *take
L          bring it out yonder   *take
L      l   bring (that dog) out of here!  /are 'bring'
               and 'take' used interchangeably?/   *take

   t o      he's playing) golf

     o      take hold

     o      let go
```

N   he is) wasting time   *loafing on the job,
               soldiering, piddling, puttering around,
               dawdling, filling, killing time, drawing pay

MS   #   I'll wait) for you   *on you

     # e c   give me another <u>chance</u>!

     # e   in good) <u>humor</u>   *in a glee, feeling frisky

     # e   I want to) get rid of him   *get shet of

                         ***

N   he gave me) a blow   *a belt, frail, job,
               jab, lick, punch, wallop, sock

N   l   he was) drunk   /derogatory and jocular terms;
               euphemisms/   *piffled, pickled, soused,
               tight, stewed, biled; he had a jag, a load

MS   m o   he acted as if (he knew it all   *he made out
               like

      m   who) swiped (my pencils?   *filched, cooned,
               thiefed, stoled, snitched, snuk

N   I didn't) <u>recognize</u> (you

N   we're going to) <u>miss</u> <u>you</u>

N   m   they used to) chat (for hours,   *jaw, jowl,
               chin, clack, chew the rag, glab, gab,
               chew the fat

MST   m o   I) don't remember   *disremember, disrecollect

   # e c   I have) written (to him   *wrote, writ

   # e   I expect an) <u>answer</u>

MS   +   will you) address (the letter?   /distinguish
               return address/   *back

                         ***

SL   he) wrote (me last week   *writ

SL   what's his <u>address</u>?

UR   rubber band   *rubber binder, binder

U   kaffeeklatch /women's informal afternoon
          party, usually with coffee/   *kaffee
          kalas, coffee party, coffee clutch

N   I bet (you ten to one   *lay

                    101

    # e c who) taught (you that?   *teached, learned,
          larnt

          we) intend (to go soon   *mean, are projectin',
          are letting on going, aim, are fixing,
          are studying on

MS   m you can) if you're a mind to   *if you want to

N   he queered (himself with   *got in wrong with,
          got in bad with, got in Dutch, got in
          hot water, cooked his goose

N   m you won't) tell on (me, will you? /terms used
          by adults; by children/   *squeal on, tattle,
          snitch

    # e   children's nicknames for one who 'tattles'
          *tongue tattler, tattle-tale, tattle-box,
          tittle-tattle, squealer, pimp, rat

    # e   pick <u>flowers</u>   *pull, gather, pluck; pretties

        m a toy   *a pretty, a play-pretty, play-toy

MS   m o I knew it!   *I jest knowed it!

                   ***

        n yarn /exaggerated story, when told?/   *cuffer

C   teacher's pet /distinguish from tattler/

N   defeat /in a game/   *trim, beat

102

```
# e c    that's the one you) gave (me    *give, gin

# e c    he) began (to talk    *begun, begin, commenced

# e c    he) ran (ashore    *run

# e c    he) came (over to see me    *come

# e c    he) saw (me go in    *see, seen, seed

# e c    the road was all) torn up    *tore up

#        put it on!

N  # e c    he) done it (last night  /past tense/    *did
```

                              ***

```
SL         put it) on (the table  /unstressed 'on'/

   1       put this away    *save it

   o       I've) put (it away  /p.ppl./
   o       I've done it

   o       thing
```

103

```
# e      nothing

# e      something

# e      it's) such a (good one

N  m o      the whole (thing

# e c    always

# e      since

# e      he did it) on purpose    *a-purpose, for purpose

# e      affirmation  /intonation and stress/    *ʔm'mm
             ʔa'ha                                    °

# e      negation  /intonation and stress/    *ʔaʔa  'ʔmʔm

MS    m      I 'think so    *I think 'so
```

***

S   <u>anything</u> *anythink

104

MS m o I am going to) ask (him *ax, ast

MS m o I) asked (him *ask, ast, ax(ed)

MS + c they) fought (all the time *fit, fout

MS m he) drew (it out *drawed

MS m o <u>hoist</u>

***

R   the dance) makes (there tonight? /record
     uses of 'make' which suggest French, Spanish,
     or other non-English language backgrounds/

S   he) went (down to the shore *goed

SL   there's too much) in (it *into
SL   it's a) <u>great</u> (thing, day, etc.

SL   he'll come) pretty soon *right soon, directly

L   I've got to) leave out (soon *leave, go
     take off

L   it) left out of (Baton Rouge at ten this morning
     /only of trains? ever of persons?/ *left

   o light out /to leave very fast/ *light a
     shuck

L   he wants to know how you can go and do that
     *why you do that

L   he could be here till yet *could've been,
     might've been

L   I asked you had you (seen him *if you'd

L   where is he (at? /pleonastic 'at'/

L   he) told me to come ask you would you (help
     him *to come and ask, ask if you would

105

L		ask them do they (live here *if they
S	o	cut it half in two /even if not in halves?/ *in two
S		don't pay him no mind *listen to him, pay attention to him
S		he didn't make me no mind *bother me
S		she'll) sweet-talk him (out of that *sweet-mouth, flatter
S	o	listen at (the bell /of things? persons?/ *to
S		peekaboo *peepeye
S		you needn't be snatched *surprised
SL		I've got) some little (oil *a little

106

SL		I'd rather do this) as (that *than
S		I'll) knock you down *introduce you
S		but yet and still (I won't go *still and all
	o	wicked and evil

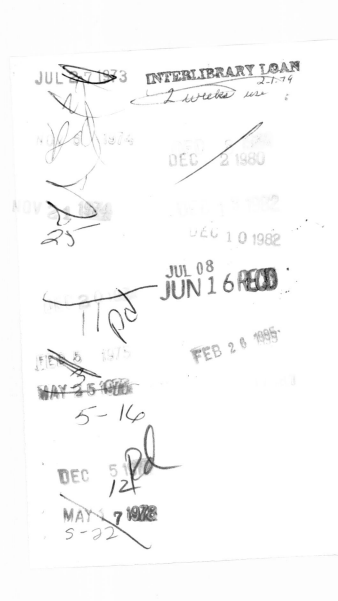